A MODERN SLAVERY

Sourcebooks in Negro History

A MODERN SLAVERY

HENRY W. NEVINSON

With an Introduction by Basil Davidson

SCHOCKEN BOOKS · NEW YORK

CONTENTS

ILLUSTRATIONS

INTRODUCTION

WHEN Henry Nevinson died in 1941 at the age of eighty-five he had become an almost legendary figure. The words are those of his friend H. N. Brailsford, whose own reputation was no otherwise when he himself died seventeen years later; and this is surely the place to recall what Brailsford meant by them and how Henry Nevinson, who turned courage and great gifts to the service of a captive world, appeared to his friends and contemporaries. Brailsford wrote long afterwards that they had first met in 1897, while Greece was fighting the Turkish empire, "when he was a correspondent on the Greek side and I a volunteer." It was a strange encounter but it led to a lifelong companionship. "I was painfully conscious that my ill-fitting uniform was ragged and dirty, and I was limping on a wounded foot. The man I met made on me, at a first glance, an impression of physical perfection. He was tall and well-proportioned; he carried himself like a soldier, and whatever he did with his body, he did well—riding and swimming, climbing and dancing.

"He had straight, clean features with blue eyes and a little pointed beard. I remember thinking at the first meeting that he carried about with him a suggestion of something Elizabethan, for he seemed older and also younger than the rest of us. He looked like Drake and he behaved like Philip Sydney. We sat talking in the great square of Athens through a long evening in May. What we said to each other I no longer remember. But I made the discovery that this handsome man, who looked like a soldier and an athlete, was also a scholar and a poet. I went on through forty years making discoveries about him. Looking back, I realize that I had as my friend one of the noblest personalities of our time. Through most of his life he fought the great powers and the big battalions. He laughed at our foibles. Against our customs, our institutions, and our rulers he was in continual rebellion. And yet I should call him the most typical Englishman of his day. He loved England with a lifelong passion. . . . If he was often in opposition, that was because he held our English ideals of freedom and humanity with more steadfastness and courage than most of us, just as he spoke and wrote our language with a keener sense for its rhythm and its beauty."

These days Nevinson is much forgotten. But this admirable re-publication of one of his best books may perhaps be taken as sufficient proof that he holds the place in history which his contemporaries—they used to call him "the Grand Duke" out of sheer affection and delight —believed was his due. *A Modern Slavery* is about Nevinson's long visit to the Portuguese colony of Angola in late 1904 and early 1905. When it was first published (in 1906) it became immediately famous with those who battled on the liberal side of life and odious to those who did not. Grim and fearful in its steady factual picture of a slave colony, the book is shot through with Nevinson's underlying belief that what was evil could be mended and what was good might yet be made to prevail. Many who read it at the time were stirred to protest, and although their pressure on the dumb ox of conformity had no great result, it is nonetheless true that nothing afterwards was ever quite the same. Nevinson had told the truth, and the truth was terrible. And once the truth was out, there flowed onward a sure small stream of memory and understanding, so that later, when others returned to the same scandal, they could find a wide hearing for what they had to say. *A Modern Slavery* is not only journalism at its highest point, a prime example to all who practice the craft of telling the truth about things as they happen, or at least of trying to tell it: this book is also a capital document in the history of modern Africa.

One reason lay in Nevinson's practical approach to the world he lived in. He believed in freedom, but not as a remote ideal. "I know Goethe's saying," he once wrote, "that there breathes so sweet a sound in the word Freedom, that we could not do without it, even if it always implied error. I know rebellion's universal anthem of '*Liberté, Liberté chérie!*' But I can form no vivid conception of Freedom apart from what I have seen. To me the word conveys nothing as a Natural Right, nothing as an abstract idea, and nothing as a symbolic woman with wings blowing a trumpet into the ears of marble captives, decoratively asleep in chains. I have learnt the reality of the thing only from the misery of its opposite, and when I hear the word Freedom I see shaggy farmers, rough with mud and storm, clad in leather cut from outstarved horses, waiting at the bottom of a watercourse, rifle in hand. Or I see a woman in rags cowering under a ruined wall while sleet hisses upon the charred and open patch of ground which was her home. Or I see a pale man and girl hurried over the snow between brown-coated soldiers with fixed bayonets, to be hacked to pieces in a barrack yard. Or I see a herd of black Africans, men and women, huddled together upon a steamer's deck, gazing like driven cattle towards the misty islands"—he was thinking of the Portuguese islands of San Thomé and Principe off the coast of Angola—"where they will toil until they die, in order that our chocolate creams may be cheap."

This practical approach may be found on every page of the compulsively readable book that follows here. A romantic he may have been: a sentimentalist never. There were many in his day who wept sweet tears of comfortable sadness on behalf of "the poor Africans," and urged the rapid consummation of colonial rule so that civilization might spread and flourish. Nevinson never did the first nor fell into the mistake of the second: he saw that what "the poor Africans" were most suffering from was precisely that kind of civilization which spreads by conquest and by "pacification." He sailed down the long west coast by way of the Bight of Benin and landed at Luanda, then as now the capital of Angola. He found it "the only place that looks like a town at all" between Moorish Tangiers and Dutch Cape Town, but full of troubles: a great deal of sleepy sickness, it appeared, and an economic crisis resulting from a collapse in cocoa prices, from the competition of Brazilian coffee and Congo rubber, and from a vast deal of sugar being turned into rum for local consumption. He learned that wars of "pacification" were still going on in the interior, and investigating these might have taken up his time had it not been for the central point of his mission. This was to find out whether it was true, as reports in Europe said, that the country was being largely run by forced labor, especially in the growing of San Thomé cocoa which was then (but not for long afterwards) Europe's principal means of making chocolate.

As it proved in the event, Nevinson was just in time to witness the last appalling period of outright slavery in Angola. Traveling through the inland plains he saw the shackles discarded by the wayside, the old bones and the new bones, the desolation of a countryside denuded of its people. Knowing his mission, slave drivers tried hard to fool or avoid him; on his return to the coast there was even an attempt to poison him. Nevinson never allowed himself to be misled or intimidated, but he also never allowed himself to indulge any particular animus against the Portuguese as such. He looked hard for any signs of Portuguese opposition to the system and for pointers to a different future. He mentions certain movements against slavery in Portugal itself, and notes a little newspaper "which appears occasionally in Luanda (*A Defeza de Angola*) in which the shame of the whole system is exposed, at all events with courage."

Copies of that little newspaper are next to impossible to find any longer—which is sad for the reputation of Portugal—but fortunately we have this book. It gives an essential part of the background to Angola today. "This is the path," he writes of the trail-scarred hillside that tilts at last to the Atlantic near Catumbela, "down which the caravans of slaves from the basin of the Upper Congo have been brought for generations, and down this path within the last three or four years the slaves were openly driven to the coast, shackled, tied together, and beaten along with whips, the trader considering himself fairly fortunate if out of his drove of human beings he brought half alive to the market. There is a notorious case in which a Portuguese trader, who still follows his calling unchecked, lost six hundred out of nine hundred on the way down."

How was this bondage imposed? And what has since become of it? When the Portuguese first arrived on these shores in the last two decades of the fifteenth century they found that the principal peoples of the coastland country, the Bakongo in the north and the Kimbundu somewhat to the south, were living in kingdoms of their own. With the rulers of these kingdoms the Portuguese struck alliances of friendship. But gradually the alliances were broken by Portuguese governors and soldiers and traders. Little by little the coastland peoples were brought under direct Portuguese rule. More and more they were drawn into the fatal work of procuring slaves for export to Brazil. The whole vast country soon became a reservoir of slave labor for Brazilian planters and mining bosses. Angola itself became a slave society. Passing through Luanda in 1666, two Italian priests found "a prodigious multitude of Blacks" who "serve as slaves to the whites, some of whom have fifty, some a hundred, two or three hundred, and even to three thousand." Misery and decay undermined all intelligent enterprise. "By the beginning of the nineteenth century," writes Mr. James Duffy, the distinguished American historian of Portuguese Africa, "the surface splendor of Luanda had begun to tarnish; the fine buildings were falling into disrepair; its streets were unattended; transportation into the interior was in a state of neglect. . . . The population of Luanda and Benguela was made up predominantly of social castaways."

Portuguese military pressure and the slave trade had meanwhile gone far to ruin the peoples of the hills and plains behind the coastland. Yet the Portuguese could establish firm control of the interior only in the second decade of the present century, and even then they met with fierce and frequent resistance. These years were marked by risings and rebellions, notably of the Ovumbundu people (or the Bailundo, as the Portuguese have usually called them) in 1902 and of the Bakongo in 1913. Having won control of the interior, the Portuguese extended their system of forced plantation labor. Then for a while there was brief improvement in the 1920's under the influence of Governor Norton de Matos, and some slight attempt to encourage new ideas. But in 1926 Dr. Salazar was hoisted to power in Lisbon by an army coup, and his regime, based as it was on the ideas of Italian fascism, returned at once to the old attitude of dictatorial contempt for Africans, who were regarded as less than human. The chattel slavery that Angola had known for so long was now confirmed under new forms of "periodical slavery," known generally as "contract labor."

Under Salazar's laws, rephrasing and reinforcing those of the past, nearly all adult male Africans—from teenagers to grandfathers—were made subject to forced labor. They were obliged "in the sacred name of work" to take service under an employer for at least six months of every year. Abuse of this obligation soon came to mean, and continued to mean, that large numbers of men were made to suffer arbitrary labor "recruitment" and long years of unbroken servitude. At the same time the laws provided that no Africans had any claim to civic rights—no access to political responsibilities, no education beyond a rudimentary stage for a small minority of children—unless they had won the status of *assimilado* ("civilized person") : by the early 1960's, nearly five centuries after the Portuguese had first reached Angola, the number of Africans who had been allowed to win this status was fewer than one in every hundred. Medical services were primitive or altogether lacking. Economic development was entirely along colonial lines, and even so pathetically small.

What all this meant for the peoples of the coast and the interior—numbering perhaps four million by the 1940's—was described in a notable report by Portugal's senior inspector of colonies, Captain Henrique Galvão, in 1947. This report was understandably suppressed by Salazar, but was published clandestinely two years later. It offers an indispensable sequel to Nevinson's report of forty-one years earlier. Galvão traveled widely in Angola. As a high official, he had access to otherwise unobtainable information. His conclusions were crushing. "I maintain," he wrote, "that health services for the natives of Angola, Monzambique, and [Portuguese] Guinea—whether paid for by Government or imposed by Government on private employers—are, with rare exceptions, non-existent." It was "not surprising that infant mortality reaches a figure of 60 per cent, and that a death rate as high as 40 per cent is not rare among workers themselves" during their periods of forced labor. He believed that Angola was rapidly nearing catastrophe.

Galvão considered that the worst aspect of the labor position lay "in the attitude of the State to the recruit-

ment of labor for private employers. Here the position is
worse in Angola than in Mozambique; because in Angola,
openly and deliberately, the State acts as recruiting agent
for labor on behalf of settlers who, as though it were
quite natural, write to the Department of Native Affairs
for 'a supply of workers.' This word 'supply' [*fornecer*]
is used indifferently of goods or of men." Denouncing
this recruitment of forced labor, Galvão concluded in
words which have since echoed around the world: "In
some ways the situation is worse than simple slavery.
Under slavery, after all, the native is bought as an ani-
mal: his owner prefers him to remain as fit as a horse or
an ox. Yet here the native is not bought—he is hired from
the State, although he is called a free man. And his employer cares little if he sickens or dies, once he is working, because when he sickens or dies his employer will
simply ask for another." This, as will be seen, was essen-
tially little different from the system that Nevinson had
found in 1904.

After Galvão made his report two contradictory but
complementary processes occurred in Angola. The oppression grew worse. But the oppressed began—for the
first time—to organize their resistance on modern political
lines. It is difficult to know by how much the oppression
grew worse, but the main facts are clear enough. The
Salazar regime embarked upon a large annual export of
poor peasants to Angola. One effect of this was to introduce cheap white labor and thereby, following the dismal
logic of such things, to strengthen the ideas and practices
of white racialism. Poor Portuguese wage-earners began
reacting against the competition of poor African wage-
earners by urging measures of discrimination against

"free" African workers and *assimilados*. At the same time the post-war boom in raw material prices raised the demand for forced plantation labor under the so-called "contract" system. According to the files of the Department of Native Affairs at Luanda, when I was there myself in 1954, there were about 379,000 Africans under "contract," or about one third of all "fit adult males." Thus there was probably more coercion than ever before. It is against this background of organized repression and impoverishment of the bulk of the people that the great rebellion of 1961 must be seen.

The first faint stirrings of resistance, far underground as yet, occurred in the early 1950's. News began circulating in Angola of the political emancipation that was taking place in some French and British colonies. The voice of an independent Africa began to be heard, muffled but insistent. African "cultural associations," formed legally at Luanda and one or two other places, turned to political discussion, cautious and heavily concealed but inspired by the belief that a time of change had come at last. Sometime in 1953 about fifty Africans sent a manifesto to the Secretariat of the United Nations, boldly signing it with their own names and setting forth their reasoned protest against the misery and terror from which they sought relief. Then in 1954 the first political parties were founded in secret. Two of these have since become important. Both were active in the preparation and prosecution of the 1961 rebellion.

None of these parties turned to violence without first having tried to achieve their end—movement toward the emancipation of Angola—by peaceful means. But it was soon clear that the Salazar regime had no intention of meeting them on any terms but those of ruthless persecution. By June, 1960, many hundreds of politically minded Africans, as well as some democratic Portuguese, were in prison or detention camps. And in that month, with profound effect on countless people in Angola, the neighboring Belgian Congo became the Congo Republic. In northern Angola the Bakongo were already well aware that their kinsmen in the ex-French Congo were beginning to run their own affairs. Now they saw their kinsmen in the ex-Belgian Congo beginning to do the same. Yet if the "French Bakongo" and the "Belgian Bakongo" were ripe for liberty, why not the "Portuguese Bakongo" as well? The scene was set for a new struggle. Thanks to Portuguese obscurantism, it was to take the path of violent revolution.

The rebellion had its first eruption on February 4, 1961, in the city of Luanda. Captain Galvão, the ex-inspector of colonies who was now in open revolt against the Salazar dictatorship, had seized the Portuguese liner *Santa Maria* and was thought to be sailing for Luanda. Perhaps it was this that touched off the attack on the São Paulo jail on February 4. In any event, the attack was made, and proved the signal for the war that soon followed. In itself the attack failed, and was answered at once by a Portuguese massacre of Africans in the "native townships" of the capital. Salazar's officials proclaimed that all was over. In fact it had only just begun.

Five weeks later, on March 15, the Bakongo of the north swung into desperate action. Small groups, which had armed and prepared themselves in previous weeks, went down to European farmsteads and villages and murdered several hundred Portuguese men, women, and children, often atrociously. (How many they killed remains in doubt: while Salazarist propaganda claims "five hundred or a thousand," the 1961 annual report of the well-informed Angola Diamond Company refers only to the death of about two hundred white men, women, and children in the first few days; whites killed since then have almost all been soldiers or armed civilians.) This grim outburst of peasant anger, matching the familiar horrors of repression with a new brutality, was the beginning of a guerrilla war that spread rapidly southward to the country of the Kimbundu and thence, southward again, to that of the Ovimbundu. "No one," commented the London *Economist* on March 25, "should feel anything but horror at this renewal of bloodshed in a part of the world that has already had a share of it this year; nor, however, should anyone be under any doubt that more will follow if the Portuguese government fails to modernize and improve its African policy."

But the Portuguese government had only one idea in its head, and that was the old one of repression. The weeks that followed the Bakongo rising were stained with a massacre of Africans which surpassed anything known for many years in any part of colonial Africa. By mid-June the British Baptist Missionary Society, drawing on its own good sources of information within the country, estimated that the Portuguese had killed some 20,000 African men, women, and children since the middle of March. They spoke of "death and disaster." They believed that the government was planning to kill many thousand more. In this forecast they were soon proved right. Widespread bombing of villages became a daily occurrence. There is strong ground for believing that napalm was used. "The cumulative evidence of returning missionaries and African refugees of the napalm bombing of villages and wholesale executions," noted the London *Sunday Times* on July 1, "is too consistent to be ignored." By the end of July nearly 100,000 Africans had fled from Angola across the frontier into the Congo. In 1962, International Red Cross figures showed a total of about 215,000 refugees in the Congo. Yet the Salazar regime behaves exactly as before.

Such are the bare facts. To understand them, and to see why so many Africans in Angola have preferred and still prefer to face death or starvation than to go on living in a Portuguese colony, there is no better way than to read what Henry Nevinson wrote about this country. His book is signally up to date.

BASIL DAVIDSON

A MODERN SLAVERY

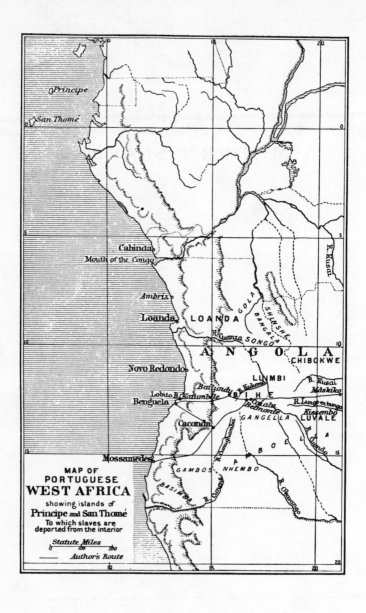

Principe

San Thome

Cabinda
Mouth of the Congo

Ambriz

Loanda   L O A N D A   G O L A

SHINSHE

BANGALA

R. Cuanza   SONGO

A N G O L A

CHIBOKWE

Novo Redondo

LUMBI

R. Kusai
Mashiko

Bailundu   R. Kukema
Lobito B.   Catumbele   **BIHE**
Benguela   Calala   R. Lungo en tunga
Belmonte   Kissembo
GANGELLA   **LUVALE**

Caconda   R. Kuango   R. Luando

A

Mossamedes   R. Kisanganga   C A M B O D

MAP OF
PORTUGUESE
WEST AFRICA
showing islands of
Principe and **San Thomé**
To which slaves are
deported from the interior

GAMBOS   NHEMBO

BASUTO   R. Cunene   R. Okavango

Statute Miles
0   100   200
—————   Author's Route

I

INTRODUCTORY

FOR miles on miles there is no break in the monotony of the scene. Even when the air is calmest the surf falls heavily upon the long, thin line of yellow beach, throwing its white foam far up the steep bank of sand. And beyond the yellow beach runs the long, thin line of purple forest—the beginning of that dark forest belt which stretches from Sierra Leone through West and Central Africa to the lakes of the Nile. Surf, beach, and forest —for two thousand miles that is all, except where some great estuary makes a gap, or where the line of beach rises to a low cliff, or where a few distant hills, leading up to Ashanti, can be seen above the forest trees.

It is not a cheerful part of the world—"the Coast." Every prospect does not please, nor is it only man that is vile. Man, in fact, is no more vile than elsewhere; but if he is white he is very often dead.

We pass in succession the white man's settlements, with their ancient names so full of tragic and miserable history—Axim, Sekundi, Cape Coast Castle, and Lagos. We see the old forts, built by Dutch and Portuguese to protect their trade in ivory and gold and the souls of men. They still gleam, white and cool as whitewash can make them, among the modern erections of tin and iron that have a meaner birth. And always, as we pass, some "old Coaster" will point to a drain or an unfinished church, and say, "That was poor Anderson's last bit." And always when we stop and the officials come off to the ship, drenched by the surf in spite of the skill of native crews, who drive the boats with rapid paddles, hissing sharply at every stroke to keep the time—always the first news is of sickness and death. Its form is brief: "Poor Smythe down—fever." "Poor Cunliffe gone—black-water." "Poor Tompkinson scuppered—natives." Every one says, "Sorry," and there's no more to be said.

It is not cheerful. The touch of fate is felt the more keenly because the white people are so few. For the most part, they know one another, at all events by classes. A soldier knows a soldier. Unless he is very military, indeed, he knows the district commissioner, and other officials as well. An official knows an official, and is quite on speaking terms with the soldiers. A trader knows a trader, and ceases to watch him with malignant jealousy when he dies. It is hard to realize how few the white men are, scattered among the black swarms of the natives. I believe that in the six-mile radius round Lagos (the largest "white" town on the Coast) the whites could not muster one hundred and fifty among the one hundred and forty thousand blacks. And in the great walled city of Abeokuta, to which the bit of railway from Lagos runs, among a black population of two hundred and five thousand, the whites could hardly make up twenty all told. So that when one white man disappears he leaves a more obvious gap than he would in a London street, and any white man may win a three days' fame by dying.

Among white women, a loss is naturally still more obvious and deplorable. Speaking generally, we may say the only white women on the Coast are nurses and missionaries. A benevolent government forbids soldiers and officials to bring their wives out. The reason given is the deadly climate, though there are other reasons, and an exception seems to be made in the case of a governor's wife. She enjoys the liberty of dying at her own discretion. But Accra, almost alone of the Coast towns, boasts the presence of two or three English ladies, and I have known men overjoyed at being ordered to appointments there. Not that they were any more devoted to the society of ladies than we all are, but they hoped for a better chance of surviving in a place where ladies live. Vain hope; in spite of cliffs and clearings, in spite of golf and polo, and ladies, too, Death counts his shadows at Accra much the same as anywhere else.

You never can tell. I once landed on a beach where it seemed that death would be the only chance of comfort in the tedious hell. On either hand the flat shore stretched away till it was lost in distance. Close behind the beach the forest swamp began. Upon the narrow ridge nine hideous houses stood in the sweltering heat, and that was all the town. The sole occupation was an exchange of palm-oil for the deadly spirit which profound knowledge of chemistry and superior technical education have enabled the Germans to produce in a more poisonous form than any other nation. The sole intellectual excitement was the arrival of the steamers with gin, rum, and newspapers. Yet in that desolation three European ladies were dwelling in apparent amity, and a volatile little Frenchman, full of the joy of life, declared he would not change that bit of beach—no, not for all the *cafés chantants* of his native Marseilles. "There is not one Commandment here!" he cried, unconsciously imitating the poet of Mandalay; and I suppose there is some comfort in having no Commandments, even where there is very little chance of breaking any.

The farther down the Coast you go the more melancholy is the scene. The thin line of yellow beach disappears. The forest comes down into the sea. The roots of the trees are never dry, and there is no firm distinction of land and water. You have reached "the Rivers," the delta of the Niger, the Circle of the mangrove swamps, in which Dante would have stuck the Arch-Traitor head downward if only he had visited this part of the world. I gained my experience of the swamps early, but it was thorough. It was about the third time I landed on the Coast. Hearing that only a few miles away there was real solid ground where strange beasts roamed, I determined to cut a path through the forest in that direction. Engaging two powerful savages armed with "matchets," or short, heavy swords, I took the plunge from a wharf which had been built with piles beside a river. At the first step I was up to my knees in black sludge, the smell of which had been accumulating since the glacial period. Perhaps the swamps are forming the coal-beds of a remote future; but in that case I am glad I did not live at Newcastle in a remote past. As in a coronation ode, there seemed no limit to the depths of sinking. One's only chance was to strike a submerged trunk not yet quite rotten enough to count as mud. Sometimes it was possible to cling to the stems or branches of standing trees, and swing over the slime without sinking deep. It was possible, but unpleasant; for stems and branches and twigs and fibres are generally

5

covered with every variety of spine and spike and hook.

In a quarter of an hour we were as much cut off from the world as on the central ocean. The air was dark with shadow, though the tree-tops gleamed in brilliant sunshine far above our heads. Not a whisper of breeze nor a breath of fresh air could reach us. We were stifled with the smell. The sweat poured from us in the intolerable heat. Around us, out of the black mire, rose the vast tree trunks, already rotting as they grew, and between the trunks was woven a thick curtain of spiky plants and of the long suckers by which the trees draw up an extra supply of water—very unnecessarily, one would have thought.

Through this undergrowth the natives, themselves often up to the middle in slime, slowly hacked a way. They are always very patient of a white man's insanity. Now and then we came to a little clearing where some big tree had fallen, rotten from bark to core. Or we came to a "creek"—one of the innumerable little watercourses which intersect the forest, and are the favorite haunt of the mud-fish, whose eyes are prominent like a frog's, and whose side fins have almost developed into legs, so that, with the help of their tails, they can run over the slime like lizards on the sand. But for them and the crocodiles and innumerable hosts of ants and slugs, the lower depths of the mangrove swamp

6

contain few living things. Parrots and monkeys inhabit the upper world where the sunlight reaches, and sometimes the deadly stillness is broken by the cry of a hawk that has the flight of an owl and fishes the creeks in the evening. Otherwise there is nothing but decay and stench and creatures of the ooze.

After struggling for hours and finding no change in the swamp and no break in the trees, I gave up the hope of that rising ground, and worked back to the main river. When at last I emerged, sopping with sweat, black with slime, torn and bleeding from the thorns, I knew that I had seen the worst that nature can do. I felt as though I had been reforming the British War Office.

It is worth while trying to realize the nature of these wet forests and mangrove swamps, for they are the chief characteristic of "the Coast," and especially of "the Rivers." Not that the whole even of southern Nigeria is swamp. Wherever the ground rises, the bush is dry. But from a low cliff, like "The Hill" at Calabar, although in two directions you may turn to solid ground where things will grow and man can live, you look south and west over miles and miles of forest-covered swamp that is hopeless for any human use. You realize then how vain is the chatter about making the Coast healthy by draining the mangrove swamps. Until the white man develops a new kind of blood and a new kind of inside, the Coast will kill him. Till

then we shall know the old Coaster by the yellow
and streaky pallor of a blood destroyed by fevers, by
a confused and uncertain memory, and by a puffi-
ness that comes from enfeebled muscle quite as often
as from insatiable thirst.

It is through swamps like these that those un-
heard-of "punitive expeditions" of ours, with a
white officer or two, a white sergeant or two, and a
handful of trusty Hausa men, have to fight their
way, carrying their Maxim and three-inch guns
upon their heads. "I don't mind as long as the
men don't sink above the fork," said the commandant of one of them to me. And it is beside these
swamps that the traders, for many short-lived generations past, have planted their "factories."

The word "factory" points back to a time when
the traders made the palm-oil themselves. The natives make nearly the whole of it now and bring it
down the rivers in casks, but the "factories" keep
their name, though they are now little more than
depots of exchange and retail trade. Formerly
they were made of the hulks of ships, anchored out
in the rivers, and fitted up as houses and stores. A
few of the hulks still remain, but of late years the
traders have chosen the firmest piece of "beach"
they could find, or else have created a "beach" by
driving piles into the slime, and on these shaky and
unwholesome platforms have erected dwelling-houses
with big verandas, a series of sheds for the stores,

and a large barn for the shop. Here the "agent" (or sometimes the owner of the business) spends his life, with one or two white assistants, a body of native "boys" as porters and boatmen, and usually a native woman, who in the end returns to her tribe and hands over her earnings in cash or goods to her chief.

The agent's working-day lasts from sunrise to sunset, except for the two hours at noon consecrated to "chop" and tranquillity. In the evening, sometimes he gambles, sometimes he drinks, but, as a rule, he goes to bed. Most factories are isolated in the river or swamp, and they are pervaded by a loneliness that can be felt. The agent's work is an exchange of goods, generally on a large scale. In return for casks of oil and bags of "kernels," he supplies the natives with cotton cloth, spirits, gunpowder, and salt, or from his retail store he sells cheap clothing, looking-glasses, clocks, knives, lamps, tinned food, and all the furniture, ornaments, and pictures which, being too atrocious even for English suburbs and provincial towns, may roughly be described as Colonial.

From the French coasts, in spite of the free-trade agreement of 1898, the British trader is now almost entirely excluded. On the Ivory Coast, Dahomey, French Congo, and the other pieces of territory which connect the enormous African possessions of France with the sea, you will hardly find a British factory left, though in one or two cases the skill and perseverance of an agent may just keep an old firm going. In the German Cameroons, British houses still do rather more than half the trade, but their existence is continually threatened. In Portuguese Angola one or two British factories cling to their old ground in hopes that times may change. In the towns of the Lower Congo the British firms still keep open their stores and shops; but the well-known policy of the royal rubber merchant, who bears on his shield a severed hand sable, has killed all real trade above Stanley Pool. In spite of all protests and regulations about the "open door," it is only in British territory that a British trader can count upon holding his own. It may be said that, considering the sort of stuff the British trader now sells, this is a matter of great indifference to the world. That may be so. But it is not a matter of indifference to the British trader, and, in reality, it is ultimately for his sake alone that our possessions in West Africa are held. Ultimately it is all a question of soap and candles.

We need not forget the growing trade in mahogany and the growing trade in cotton. We may take account of gold, ivory, gums, and kola, besides the minor trades in fruits, yams, red peppers, millet, and the beans and grains and leaves which make a native market so enlivening to a botanist. But, after all, palm-oil and kernels are the things that count, and palm-oil and kernels come to soap and candles in the end. It is because our dark and dirty little island needs such quantities of soap and candles that we have extended the blessings of European civilization to the Gold Coast and the Niger, and beside the lagoons of Lagos and the rivers of Calabar have placed our barracks, hospitals, mad-houses, and prisons. It is for this that district commissioners hold their courts of British justice and officials above suspicion improve the perspiring hour by adding up sums. For this the natives trim the forest into golf-links. For this devoted teachers instruct the Fantee boys and girls in the length of Irish rivers and the order of Napoleon's campaigns. For this the director of public works dies at his drain and the officer at a palisade gets an iron slug in his stomach. For this the bugles of England blow at Sokoto, and the little plots of white crosses stand conspicuous at every clearing.

That is the ancestral British way of doing things. It is for the sake of the trade that the whole affair is ostensibly undertaken and carried on. Yet the officer and the official up on "The Hill" quietly ignore the trader at the foot, and are dimly conscious of very different aims. The trader's very existence depends upon the skill and industry of the natives. Yet the trader quietly ignores the native, or speaks of him only as a lazy swine who ought to

be enslaved as much as possible. And all the time
the trader's own government is administering a singularly equal justice, and has, within the last three
years, declared slavery of every kind at an end forever.

In the midst of all such contradictions, what is
to be the real relation of the white races to the black
races? That is the ultimate problem of Africa.
We need not think it has been settled by a century's
noble enthusiasm about the Rights of Man and
Equality in the sight of God. Outside a very small
and diminishing circle in England and America,
phrases of that kind have lost their influence, and
for the men who control the destinies of Africa
they have no meaning whatever. Neither have
they any meaning for the native. He knows perfectly well that the white people do not believe
them.

The whole problem is still before us, as urgent
and as uncertain as it has ever been. It is not
solved. What seemed a solution is already obso-
lete. The problem will have to be worked through
again from the start. Some of the factors have
changed a little. Laws and regulations have been
altered. New and respectable names have been invented. But the real issue has hardly changed at
all. It has become a part of the world-wide issue
of capital, but the question of African slavery still
abides.

INTRODUCTORY

We may, of course, draw distinctions. The old-fashioned export of human beings as a reputable and staple industry, on a level with the export of palm-oil, has disappeared from the Coast. Its old headquarters were at Lagos; and scattered about that district and in Nigeria and up the Congo one can still see the remains of the old barracoons, where the slaves were herded for sale or shipment. In passing up the rivers you may suddenly come upon a large, square clearing. It is overgrown now, but the bush is not so high and thick as the surrounding forest, and palms take the place of the mangrove-trees. Sometimes a little Ju-ju house is built by the water's edge, with fetiches inside; and perhaps the natives have placed it there with some dim sense of expiation. For the clearing is the site of an old barracoon, and misery has consecrated the soil. Such things leave a perpetual heritage of woe. The English and the Portuguese were the largest slave-traders upon the Coast, and it is their descendants who are still paying the heaviest penalty. But that ancient kind of slave-trade may for the present be set aside. The British gun-boats have made it so difficult and so unlucrative that slavery has been driven to take subtler forms, against which gun-boats have hitherto been powerless.

We may draw another distinction still. Quite different from the plantation slavery under European control, for the profit of European capitalists,

is the domestic slavery that has always been practised among the natives themselves. Legally, this
form of slavery was abolished in Nigeria by a roc-
lamation of 1901, but it still exists in spite of the
law, and is likely to exist for many years, even in
British possessions. It is commonly spoken of as
domestic slavery, but perhaps tribal slavery would
be the better word. Or the slave might be compared to the serf of feudal times. He is nominally
the property of the chief, and may be compelled to
give rather more than half his days to work for the
tribe. Even under the Nigerian enactment, he cannot leave his district without the chief's consent,
and he must continue to contribute something to
the support of the family. But in most cases a
slave may purchase his freedom if he wishes, and it
frequently happens that a slave becomes a chief
himself and holds slaves on his own account.

It is one of those instances in which law is ahead
of public custom. Most of the existing domestic
slaves do not wish for further freedom, for if their
bond to the chief were destroyed, they would lose
the protection of the tribe. They would be friend-
less and outcast, with no home, no claim, and no
appeal. "Soon be head off," said a native, in trying to explain the dangers of sudden freedom. At
Calabar I came across a peculiar instance. Some
Scottish missionaries had carefully trained up a
native youth to work with them at a mission. They

had taught him the height of Chimborazo, the cost of papering a room, leaving out the fireplace, and the other things which we call education because we can teach nothing else. They had even taught him the intricacies of Scottish theology. But just as he was ready primed for the ministry, an old native stepped in and said: "No; he is my slave. I beg to thank you for educating him so admirably. But he seems to me better suited for the government service than for the cure of souls. So he shall enter a government office and comfort my declining years with half his income."

The elderly native had himself been educated by the mission, and that added a certain irony to his claim. When I told the acting governor of the case, he thought such a thing could not happen in these days, because the youth could have appealed to the district commissioner, and the old man's claim would have been disallowed at law. That may be so; and yet I have not the least doubt that the account I received was true. Law was in advance of custom, that was all, and the people followed custom, as people always do.

Even where there is no question of slave-ownership, the power of the chiefs is often despotic. If a chief covets a particularly nice canoe, he can purchase it by compelling his wives and children to work for the owner during so many days. Or take the familiar instance of the "Krooboys." The

Kroo coast is nominally part of Liberia, but as the
Liberian government is only a fit subject for comic
opera, the Kroo people remain about the freest and
happiest in Africa. Their industry is to work the
cargo of steamers that go down the Coast. They
get a shilling a day and "chop," and the only condition they make is to return to "we country"
within a year at furthest. Before the steamer stops
off the Coast and sounds her hooter the sea is covered with canoes. The captain sends word to the
chief of the nearest village that he wants, say, fifty
"boys." After two or three hours of excited pal-
aver on shore, the chief selects fifty boys, and they
are sent on board under a headman. When they
return, they give the chief a share of their earnings
as a tribute for his care of the tribe and village in
their absence. This is a kind of feudalism, but it
has nothing to do with slavery, especially as there
is a keen competition among the boys to serve.
When a woman who has been hired as a white man's
concubine is compelled to surrender her earnings
to the chief, we may call it a survival of tribal slavery, or of the patriarchal system, if you will. But
when, as happens, for instance, in Mozambique, the
agents of capitalists bribe the chiefs to force laborers to the Transvaal mines, whether they wish
to go or not, we may disguise the truth as we like
under talk about "the dignity of labor" and "the
value of discipline," but, as a matter of fact, we are

on the downward slope to the new slavery. It is easy to see how one system may become merged into the other without any very obvious breach of native custom. But, nevertheless, the distinction is profound. As Mr. Morel has said in his admirable book on *The Affairs of West Africa*, between the domestic servitude of Nigeria and plantation slavery under European supervision there is all the difference in the world. The object of the present series of sketches is to show, by one particular instance, the method under which this plantation slavery is now being carried on, and the lengths to which it is likely to develop.

"In the region of the Unknown, Africa is the Absolute." It was one of Victor Hugo's prophetic sayings a few years before his death, when he was pointing out to France her road of empire. And in a certain sense the saying is still true. In spite of all the explorations, huntings, killings, and gospels, Africa remains the unknown land, and the nations of Europe have hardly touched the edge of its secrets. We still think of "black people" in lumps and blocks. We do not realize that each African has a personality as important to himself as each of us is in his own eyes. We do not even know why the mothers in some tribes paint their babies on certain days with stripes of red and black, or why an African thinks more of his mother than we think of lovers. If we ask for the hidden meaning of a Ju-ju, or of some slow and hypnotizing dance, the native's eyes are at once covered with a film like a seal's, and he gazes at us in silence. We know nothing of the ritual of scars or the significance of initiation. We profess to believe that external nature is symbolic and that the universe is full of spiritual force; but we cannot enter for a moment into the African mind, which really believes in the spiritual side of nature. We talk a good deal about our sense of humor, but more than any other races we despise the Africans, who alone out of all the world possess the same power of laughter as ourselves.

In the higher and spiritual sense, Victor Hugo's saying remains true—"In the region of the Unknown, Africa is the Absolute." But now for the first time in history the great continent lies open to Europe. Now for the first time men of science have traversed it from end to end and from side to side. And now for the first time the whole of it, except Abyssinia, is partitioned among the great white nations of the world. Within fifty years the greatest change in all African history has come. The white races possess the Dark Continent for their own, and what they are going to do with it is now one of the greatest problems before mankind. It is a small but very significant section of this problem which I shall hope to illustrate in my investigations.

AN AFRICAN SWAMP

THE "KROOBOYS" WORKING A SHIP ALONG THE COAST

NATIVES IN CHARACTERISTIC DRESS

PLANTER'S HOUSE ON AN ANGOLA ESTATE

FIRST MAIL-STEAMER AT LOBITO BAY

END OF THE GREAT SLAVE ROUTE AT KATUMBELLA

BIHÉAN MUSICIANS

CROSSING THE CUANZA

NATIVES BURNING GRASS FOR SALT

SKELETON OF SLAVE ON A PATH THROUGH THE HUNGRY
COUNTRY

A CHIBOKWE WOMAN AND HER FETICHES

ON THE WAY TO THE COAST

CARRIERS' REST-HUTS

"ALL DAY LONG THEY LIE ABOUT THE LOWER DECK"

SLAVE QUARTERS ON A PLANTATION

SLAVES WAITING FOR RATIONS ON SUNDAY

II

PLANTATION SLAVERY ON THE MAINLAND

LOANDA is much disquieted in mind. The town is really called St. Paul de Loanda, but it has dropped its Christian name, just as kings drop their surnames. Between Moorish Tangiers and Dutch Cape Town, it is the only place that looks like a town at all. It has about it what so few African places have—the feeling of history. We are aware of the centuries that lie behind its present form, and we feel in its ruinous quays the record of early Portuguese explorers and of the Dutch settlers.

In the mouldering little church of Our Lady of Salvation, beside the beach where native women wash, there exists the only work of art which this side of Africa can show. The church bears the date of 1664, but the work of art was perhaps ordered a few years before that, while the Dutch were holding the town, for it consists of a series of pictures in blue-and-white Dutch tiles, evidently representing scenes in Loanda's history. In some cases the tiles have fallen down, and been stuck on again by natives in the same kind of chaos in which natives would rearrange the stars. But in one picture a gallant old ship is seen laboring in a tempest; in another a gallant young horseman in pursuit of a stag is leaping over a cliff into the sea; and in the third a thin square of Christian soldiers, in broad-brimmed hats, braided tail-coats, and silk stockings, is being attacked on every side by a black and unclad host of savages with bows and arrows. The Christians are ranged round two little cottages which must signify the fort of Loanda at the time. Two little cannons belch smoke and lay many black figures low. The soldiers are firing their muskets into the air, no doubt in the hope that the height of the trajectory will bring the bullets down in the neighborhood of the foe, though the opposing forces are hardly twenty yards apart. The natives in one place have caught hold of a priest and are about to exalt him to martyrdom, but I think none of the Christian soldiers have fallen. In defiance of the cannibal king, who bears a big sword and is twice the size of his followers, the Christian general grasps his standard in the middle of the square, and, as in the shipwreck and the hunting scene, Our Lady of Salvation watches serenely from the clouds, conscious of her power to save.

Unhappily there is no inscription, and we can only say that the scene represents some hard-won battle of long ago — some crisis in the miserable conflict of black and white. Since the days of those two cottages and a flag, Loanda has grown into a city that would hardly look out of place upon the Mediterranean shore. It has something now of the Mediterranean air, both in its beauty and its decay. In front of its low red and yellow cliffs a long spit of sand-bank forms a calm lagoon, at the entrance of which the biggest war-ships can lie. The sandy rock projecting into the lagoon is crowned by a Vauban fortress whose bastions and counter-scarps would have filled Uncle Toby's heart with joy. They now defend the exiled prisoners from Portugal, but from the ancient embrasures a few old guns, some rusty, some polished with blacking, still puff their salutes to foreign men-of-war, or to new governors on their arrival. In blank-cartridge the Portuguese War Depatment shows no economy. If only ball-cartridge were as cheap, the mind of Loanda would be less disquieted.

There is an upper and a lower town. From the fortress the cliff, though it crumbles down in the centre, swings round in a wide arc to the cemetery, and on the cliff are built the governor's palace, the bishop's palace, a few ruined churches that once belonged to monastic orders, and the fine big hospital, an expensive present from a Portuguese queen. Over the flat space between the cliff and the lagoon the lower town has grown up, with a cathedral, custom-house, barracks, stores, and two restaurants. The natives live scattered about in

houses and huts, but they have chiefly spread at
random over the flat, high ground behind the cliff.
As in a Turkish town, there is much ruin and plenty
of space. Over wide intervals of ground you will
find nothing but a broken wall and a century of
rubbish. Many enterprises may be seen growing
cold in death. There are gardens which were meant
to be botanical. There is an observatory which
may be scientific still, for the wind-gage spins.
There is an immense cycle track which has delighted
no cyclist, unless, indeed, the contractor cycles.
There are bits of pavement that end both ways in
sand. There is a ruin that was intended for a hotel.
There is a public band which has played the same
tunes in the same order three times a week since the
childhood of the oldest white inhabitant. There is
a technical school where no pupil ever went. There
is a vast municipal building which has never received its windows, and whose tower serves as a
monument to the last sixpence. There are oil-lamps
which were made for gas, and there is one drain,
fit to poison the multitudinous sea.

So the city lies, bankrupt and beautiful. She is
beautiful because she is old, and because she built
her roofs with tiles, before corrugated iron came to
curse the world. And she is bankrupt for various
reasons, which, as I said, are now disquieting her
mind. First there is the war. Only last autumn
a Portuguese expedition against a native tribe was

cut to pieces down in the southern Mossamedes district, not far from the German frontier, where also a war is creeping along. No Lady of Salvation now helped the thin Christian square, and some three hundred whites and blacks were left there dead. So things stand. Victorious natives can hardly be allowed to triumph in victory over whites, but how can a bankrupt province carry on war? A new governor has arrived, and, as I write, everything is in doubt, except the lack of money. How are safety, honor, and the value of the milreis note to be equally maintained?

But there is an uneasy consciousness that the lack of money, the war itself, and other distresses are all connected with a much deeper question that keeps on reappearing in different forms. It is the question of "contract labor." Cheap labor of some sort is essential, if the old colony is to be preserved. There was a time when there was plenty of labor and to spare—so much to spare that it was exported in profitable ship-loads to Havana and Brazil, while the bishop sat on the wharf and christened the slaves in batches. But, as I have said, that source of income was cut off by British gun-boats some fifty years ago, and is lost, perhaps forever. And in the mean time the home supply of labor has been lamentably diminished; for the native population, the natural cultivators of the country, have actually decreased in number, and other causes have contributed to raise their price above the limit of "economic value."

Their numbers have decreased, because the whole country, always exposed to small-pox, has been suffering more and more from the diseases which alcoholism brings or leaves, and, like most of tropical Africa, it has been devastated within the last twenty or thirty years by this new plague to humanity, called "the sleeping - sickness." Men of science are undecided still as to the cause. They are now inclined to connect it with the tsetse-fly, long known in parts of Africa as the destroyer of all domesticated animals, but hitherto suppoed to be harmless to man, whether domesticated or wild. No one yet knows, and we can only describe its course from the observed cases. It begins with an unwillingness to work, an intense desire to sit down and do nothing, so that the lowest and most laborious native becomes quite aristocratic in his habits. The head then keeps nodding forward, and intervals of profound sleep supervene. Control over the expression of emotion is lost, so that the patient laughs or cries without cause. This has been a very marked symptom among the children I have seen. In some the great tears kept pouring down; others could not stop laughing. The muscles twitch of themselves, and the glands at the back of the neck swell up. Then the appetite fails, and in the cases I have seen there is extreme wasting, as from famine. Sometimes, however, the body swells all over, and the natives call this kind "the Baobab," from the name of the enormous and disproportioned tree which abounds here, and always looks as if it suffered from elephantiasis, like so many of the natives themselves. Often there is an intense desire to smoke, but when the pipe is lit the patient drops it with indifference. Then come fits of bitter cold, and during these fits patients have been known to fall into the fire and allow themselves to be burned to death. Towards the end, violent trembling comes on, followed by delirium and an unconsciousness which may continue for about the final fortnight. The disease lasts from six to eight months; sometimes a patient lives a year. But hitherto there has been no authenticated instance of recovery. Of all diseases, it is perhaps the only one which up to now counts its dead by cent per cent. It attacks all ages between five years and forty, and even those limits are not quite fixed. It so happens that most of the cases I have yet seen in the country have been children, but that may be accidental. For a long time it was thought that white people were exempt. But that is not so. They are apparently as liable to the sickness as the natives, and there are white patients suffering from it now in the Loanda hospital.

My reason for now dwelling upon the disease which has added a new terror to Africa is its effect upon the labor-supply. It is very capricious in its visitation. Sometimes it will cling to one side of a river and leave the other untouched. But when it appears it often sweeps the population off the face of the earth, and there are places in Angola which lately were large native towns, but are now going back to desert. So people are more than ever wanted to continue the cultivation of such land as has been cultivated, and, unhappily, it is now more than ever essential that the people should be cheap. The great days when fortunes were made in coffee, or when it was thought that cocoa would save the country, are over. Prices have sunk. Brazil has driven out Angola coffee. San Thomé has driven out the cocoa. The Congo is driving out the rubber, and the sugar-cane is grown only for the rum that natives drink—not a profitable industry from the point of view of national economics. Many of the old plantations have come to grief. Some have been amalgamated into companies with borrowed capital. Some have been sold for a song. None is prosperous; but people still think that if only "contract labor" were cheaper and more plentiful, prosperity would return. As it is, they see all the best labor draughted off to the rich island of San Thomé, never to return, and that is another reason why the mind of Loanda is much disquieted.

I do not mean that the anxiety about the "contract labor" is entirely a question of cash. The

Portuguese are quite as sensitive and kindly as other people. Many do not like to think that the "serviçaes" or "contrahidos," as they are called, are, in fact, hardly to be distinguished from the slaves of the cruel old times. Still more do not like to hear the most favored province of the Portuguese Empire described by foreigners as a slave state. There is a strong feeling about it in Portugal also, I believe, and here in Angola it is the chief subject of conversation and politics. The new governor is thought to be an "antislavery" man. A little newspaper appears occasionally in Loanda (*A Defeza de Angola*) in which the shame of the whole system is exposed, at all events with courage. The paper is not popular with the official or governing classes. No courageous newspaper ever can be; for the official person is born with a hatred of reform, because reform means trouble. But the paper is read none the less. There is a feeling about the question which I can only describe again as disquiet. It is partly conscience, partly national reputation; partly also it is the knowledge that under the present system San Thomé gets all the advantage, and the mainland is being drained of laborers in order that the island's cocoa may abound.

Legally the system is quite simple and looks innocent enough. Legally it is laid down that a native and a would-be employer come before a magistrate or other representative of the Curator-

General of Angola. and enter into a free and voluntary contract for so much work in return for so much pay. By the wording of the contract the native declares that "he has come of his own free will to contract for his services under the terms and according to the forms required by the law of April 29, 1875, the general regulation of November 21, 1878, and the special clauses relating to this province."

The form of contract continues:

1. The laborer contracts and undertakes to render all such [domestic, agricultural, etc.] services as his employer may require.

2. He binds himself to work nine hours on all days that are not sanctified by religion, with an interval of two hours for rest, and not to leave the service of the employer without permission, except in order to complain to the authorities.

3. This contract to remain in force for five complete years.

4. The employer binds himself to pay the monthly wages of ——, with food and clothing.

Then follow the magistrate's approval of the contract, and the customary conclusion about "signed, sealed, and delivered in the presence of the following witnesses." The law further lays it down that the contract may be renewed by the wish of both parties at the end of five years, that the magistrates should visit the various districts and see that the contracts are properly observed and renewed, and that all children born to the laborers, whether man or woman, during the time of his or her contract shall be absolutely free.

Legally, could any agreement look fairer and more innocent ? Or could any government have better protected a subject population in the transition from recognized slavery to free labor? Even apart from the splendor of legal language, laws often seem divine. But let us see how the whole thing works out in human life.

An agent, whom for the sake of politeness we may call a labor merchant, goes wandering about among the natives in the interior—say seven or eight hundred miles from the coast. He comes to the chief of a tribe, or, I believe, more often, to a little group of chiefs, and, in return for so many grown men and women, he offers the chiefs so many smuggled rifles, guns, and cartridges, so many bales of calico, so many barrels of rum. The chiefs select suitable men and women, very often one of the tribe gives in his child to pay off an old debt, the bargain is concluded, and off the party goes. The labor merchant leads it away for some hundreds of miles, and then offers its members to employers as contracted laborers. As commission for his own services in the transaction, he may receive about fifteen or twenty pounds for a man or a woman, and about five pounds for a child. According to law, the laborer is then brought before a magistrate and duly signs the above contract with his or her new master. He signs, and the benevolent law is satisfied. But what does the native know or care about "freedom of contract" or "the general regulation of November 21, 1878"? What does he know about nine hours a day and two hours rest and the days sanctified by religion? Or what does it mean to him to be told that the contract terminates at the end of five years? He only knows that he has fallen into the hands of his enemies, that he is being given over into slavery to the white man, that if he runs away he will be beaten, and even if he could escape to his home, all those hundreds of miles across the mountains, he would probably be killed, and almost certainly be sold again. In what sense does such a man enter into a free contract for his labor? In what sense, except according to law, does his position differ from a slave's? And the law does not count; it is only life that counts.

I do not wish at present to dwell further upon this original stage in the process of the new slave-trade, for I have not myself yet seen it at work. I only take my account from men who have lived long in the interior and whose word I can trust. I may be able to describe it more fully when I have been farther into the interior myself. But now I will pass to a stage in the system which I have seen with my own eyes—the plantation stage, in which the contract system is found in full working order.

For about a hundred miles inland from Loanda, the country is flattish and bare and dry, though there are occasional rivers and a sprinkling of trees. A coarse grass feeds a few cattle, but the chief product is the cassava, from which the natives knead a white food, something between rice and flour. As you go farther, the land grows like the "low veldt" in the Transvaal, and it has the same peculiar and unwholesome smell. By degrees it becomes more mountainous and the forest grows thick, so that the little railway seems to struggle with the undergrowth almost as much as with the inclines. That little railway is perhaps the only evidence of "progress" in the province after three or four centuries. It is paid for by Lisbon, but a train really does make the journey of about two hundred and fifty miles regularly in two days, resting the engine for the night. To reach a plantation you must get out on the route and make your way through the forest by one of those hardly perceptible "bush paths" which are the only roads. Along these paths, through flag-grasses ten feet high, through jungle that closes on both sides like two walls, up mountains covered with forest, and down valleys where the water is deep at this wet season, every bit of merchandise, stores, or luggage must be carried on the heads of natives, and every yard of the journey has to be covered on foot.

After struggling through the depths of the woods

in this way for three or four hours, we climbed a
higher ridge of mountain and emerged from the
dense growth to open summits of rock and grass.
Far away to the southeast a still higher mountain
range was visible, and I remembered, with what
writers call a momentary thrill, that from this quarter of the compass Livingstone himself had made
his way through to Loanda on one of his greatest journeys. Below the mountain edge on which
I stood lay the broad valley of the plantation,
surrounded by other hills and depths of forest.
The low white casa, with its great barns and out-
houses, stood in the middle. Close by its side were
the thatched mud huts of the work-people, the doors
barred, the little streets all empty and silent, because
the people were all at work, and the children that
were too small to work and too big to be carried
were herded together in another part of the yards.
From the house, in almost every direction, the valleys of cultivated ground stretched out like fingers,
their length depending on the shape of the ground
and on the amount of water which could be turned
over them by ditch-canals.

It was a plantation on which everything that will
grow in this part of Africa was being tried at once.
There were rows of coffee, rows of cocoa - plant,
woods of bananas, fields of maize, groves of sugar-
cane for rum. On each side of the paths mango-
trees stood in avenues, or the tree which the parlors

of Camden Town know as the India-rubber plant, though in fact it is no longer the chief source of African rubber. A few other plants and fruits were cultivated as well, but these were the main produce.

The cultivation was admirable. Any one who knows the fertile parts of Africa will agree that the great difficulty is not to make things grow, but to prevent other things from growing. The abundant growth chokes everything down. An African forest is one gigantic struggle for existence, and an African field becomes forest as soon as you take your eyes off it. But on the plantation the ground was kept clear and clean. The first glance told of the continuous and persistent labor that must be used. And as I was thinking of this and admiring the result, suddenly I came upon this continuous and persistent labor in the flesh.

It was a long line of men and women, extended at intervals of about a yard, like a company of infantry going into action. They were clearing a coffee-plantation. Bent double over the work, they advanced slowly across the ground, hoeing it up as they went. To the back of nearly every woman clung an infant, bound on by a breadth of cotton cloth, after the African fashion, while its legs straddled round the mother's loins. Its head lay between her shoulders, and bumped helplessly against her back as she struck the hoe into the ground,

Most of the infants were howling with discomfort and exhaustion, but there was no pause in the work. The line advanced persistently and in silence. The only interruption was when a loin-cloth had to be tightened up, or when one of the little girls who spend the day in fetching water passed along the line with her pitcher. When the people had drunk, they turned to the work again, and the only sound to be heard was the deep grunt or sigh as the hoe was brought heavily down into the mass of tangled grass and undergrowth between the rows of the coffee-plants.

Five or six yards behind the slowly advancing line, like the officers of a company under fire, stood the overseers, or gangers, or drivers of the party. They were white men, or three parts white, and were dressed in the traditional planter style of big hat, white shirt, and loose trousers. Each carried an eight-foot stick of hard wood, whitewood, pointed at the ends, and the look of those sticks quite explained the thoroughness and persistency of the work, as well as the silence, so unusual among the natives whether at work or play.

At six o'clock a big bell rang from the casa, and all stopped working instantly. They gathered up their hoes and matchets (large, heavy knives), put them into their baskets, balanced the baskets on their heads, and walked silently back to their little gathering of mud huts. The women unbarred the

doors, put the tools away, kindled the bits of fire-
wood they had gathered on the path from work, and
made the family meal. Most of them had to go first
to a large room in the casa where provisions are
issued. Here two of the gangers preside over the
two kinds of food which the plantation provides—
flour and dried fish (a great speciality of Angola,
known to British sailors as "stinkfish"). Each
woman goes up in turn and presents a zinc disk to
a ganger. The disk has a hole through it so that it
may be carried on a string, and it is stamped with
the words "Fazenda de Paciencia 30 Reis," let us
say, or "Paciencia Plantation $1\frac{1}{2}d$." The number
of reis varies a little. It is sometimes forty-five,
sometimes higher. In return for her disks, the
woman receives so much flour by weight, or a slab
of stinkfish, as the case may be. She puts them in
her basket and goes back to cook. The man, mean-
time, has very likely gone to the shop next door
and has exchanged his disk for a small glass of the
white sugar-cane rum, which, besides women and
occasional tobacco, is his only pleasure. But the
shop, which is owned by the plantation and worked
by one of the overseers, can supply cotton cloth, a
few tinned meats, and other things if desired, also
in exchange for the disks.

The casa and the mud huts are soon asleep. At
half-past four the big bell clangs again. At five it
clangs again. Men and women hurry out and

range themselves in line before the casa, coughing horribly and shivering in the morning air. The head overseer calls the roll. They answer their queer names. The women tie their babies on to their backs again. They balance the hoe and matchet in the basket on their heads, and pad away in silence to the spot where the work was left off yesterday. At eleven the bell clangs again, and they come back to feed. At twelve it clangs again, and they go back to work. So day follows day without a break, except that on Sundays ("days sanctified by religion") the people are allowed, in some plantations, to work little plots of ground which are nominally their own.

"No change, no pause, no hope." That is the sum of plantation life. So the man or woman known as a "contract laborer" toils, till gradually or suddenly death comes, and the poor, worn-out body is put to rot. Out in the forest you come upon the little heap of red earth under which it lies. On the top of the heap is set the conical basket of woven grasses which was the symbol of its toil in life, and now forms its only monument. For a fortnight after death the comrades of the dead think that the spirit hovers uneasily about the familiar huts. They dance and drink rum to cheer themselves and it. When the fortnight is over, the spirit is dissolved into air, and all is just as though the slave had never been.

There is no need to be hypocritical or sentimental about it. The fate of the slave differs little from the fate of common humanity. Few men or women have opportunity for more than working, feeding, getting children, and death. If any one were to maintain that the plantation life is not in reality worse than the working-people's life in most of our manufacturing towns, or in such districts as the Potteries, the Black Country, and the Isle of Dogs, he would have much to say. The same argument was the only one that counted in defence of the old slavery in the West Indies and the Southern States, and it will have to be seriously met again now that slavery is reappearing under other names. A man who has been bought for money is at least of value to his master. In return for work he gets his mud hut, his flour, his stinkfish, and his rum. The driver with his eight-foot stick is not so hideous a figure as the British overseer with his system of blackmail; and as for cultivation of the intellect and care of the soul, the less we talk about such things the better.

In this account I only mean to show that the difference between the "contract labor" of Angola, and the old-fashioned slavery of our grandfathers' time is only a difference of legal terms. In life there is no difference at all. The men and women whom I have described as I saw them have all been bought from their enemies, their chiefs, or their parents; they have either been bought themelves or were the children of people who had been bought. The legal contract, if it had been made at all, had not been observed, either in its terms or its renewal. The so-called pay by the plantation tokens is not pay at all, but a form of the "truck" system at its very worst. So far from the children being free, they now form the chief labor supply of the plantation, for the demand for "serviçaes" in San Thomé has raised the price so high that the Angola plantations could not carry on at all without the little swarms of children that are continually growing up on the estates. Sometimes, as I have heard, two or three of the men escape, and hide in the crowd at Loanda or set up a little village far away in the forest. But the risk is great; they have no money and no friends. I have not heard of a runaway laborer being prosecuted for breach of contract. As a matter of fact, the fiction of the contract is hardly even considered. But when a large plantation was sold the other day, do you suppose the contract of each laborer was carefully examined, and the length of his future service taken into consideration? Not a bit of it. The laborers went in block with the estate. Men, women, and children, they were handed over to the new owners, and became their property just like the houses and trees.

Portuguese planters are not a bit worse than other men, but their position is perilous. The owner or agent lives in the big house with three or four white or whitey-brown overseers. They are remote from all equal society, and they live entirely free from any control or public opinion that they care about. Under their absolute and unquestioned power are men and women, boys and girls—let us say two hundred in all. We may even grant, if we will, that the Portuguese planters are far above the average of men. Still I say that if they were all Archbishops of Canterbury, it would not be safe for them to be intrusted with such powers as these over the bodies and souls of men and women.

III

DOMESTIC SLAVERY ON THE MAINLAND

SOME two hundred miles south of St. Paul de Loanda, you come to a deep and quiet inlet, called Lobito Bay. Hitherto it has been desert and unknown — a spit of waterless sand shutting in a basin of the sea at the foot of barren and waterless hills. But in twenty years' time Lobito Bay may have become famous as the central port of the whole west coast of Africa, and the starting-place for traffic with the interior. For it is the base of the railway scheme known as the "Robert Williams Concession," which is intended to reach the ancient copper-mines of the Katanga district in the extreme south of the Congo State, and so to unite with the "Tanganyika Concession." It would thus connect the west coast traffic with the great lakes and the east. A branch line might also turn off at some point along the high and flat watershed between the Congo and Zambesi basins, and join the Cape Town railway near Victoria Falls. Possibly before the Johannesburg gold is exhausted, passengers from London to the Transvaal will address their luggage "viâ Lobito Bay."

But this is only prophecy. What is certain is that on January 5, 1905, a mail-steamer was for the first time warped alongside a little landing - stage of lighters, in thirty-five feet of water, and I may go down to fame as the first man to land at the future port. What I found were a few laborers' huts, a tent, a pile of sleepers, a tiny engine puffing over a mile or two of sand, and a large Portuguese custom-house with an eye to possibilities. I also found an indomitable English engineer, engaged in doing all the work with his own hands, to the entire satisfaction of the native laborers, who encouraged him with smiles.

At present the railway, which is to transform the conditions of Central Africa, runs as a little tramline for about eight miles along the sand to Katumbella. There it has something to show in the shape of a great iron bridge, which crosses the river with a single span. The day I was there the engineers were terrifying the crocodiles by knocking away the wooden piles used in the construction, and both natives and Portuguese were awaiting the collapse of the bridge with the pleasurable excitement of people who await a catastrophe that does not concern themselves. But, to the general disappointment, the last prop was knocked away and the bridge still stood. It was amazing. It was contrary to the traditions of Africa and of Portugal.

Katumbella itself is an old town, with two old forts, a dozen trading-houses, and a river of singular beauty, winding down between mountains. It is important because it stands on the coast at the end of the carriers' foot-path, which has been for centuries the principal trade route between the west and the interior. One sees that path running in white lines far over the hills behind the town, and up and down it black figures are continually passing with loads upon their heads. They bring rubber, beeswax, and a few other products of lands far away. They take back enamelled ware, rum, salt, and the bales of cotton cloth from Portugal and Manchester which, together with rum, form the real coinage and standard of value in Central Africa, salt being used as the small change. The path ends, vulgarly enough, at an oil-lamp in the chief street of Katumbella. Yet it is touched by the tragedy of human suffering. For this is the end of that great slave route which Livingstone had to cross on his first great journey, but otherwise so carefully avoided. This is the path down which the caravans of slaves from the basin of the Upper Congo have been brought for generations, and down this path within the last three or four years the slaves were openly driven to the coast, shackled, tied together, and beaten along with whips, the trader con-

sidering himself fairly fortunate if out of his drove
of human beings he brought half alive to the market. There is a notorious case in which a Portuguese trader, who still follows his calling unchecked,
lost six hundred out of nine hundred on the way
down. At Katumbella the slaves were rested, sort-
ed out, dressed, and then taken on over the fifteen
miles to Benguela, usually disguised as ordinary
carriers. The traffic still goes on, almost unchecked.
But of that ancient route from Bihé to the coast I
shall write later on, for by this path I hope to come
when I emerge from the interior and catch sight of
the sea again between the hills.

As to the town of Benguela, there is something
South African about it. Perhaps it comes from the
eucalyptus-trees, the broad and sandy roads ending
in scrubby waste, and the presence of Boer transport-
riders with their ox-wagons from southern Angola.
But the place is, in fact, peculiarly Portuguese.
Next to Loanda, it is the most important town in
the colony, and for years it was celebrated as the
very centre of the slave-trade with Brazil. In the
old days when Great Britain was the enthusiastic op-
ponent of slavery in every form, some of her men-
of-war were generally hanging about off Benguela
on the watch. They succeeded in making the trade
difficult and unlucrative; but we have all become
tamer now and more ready to show consideration
for human failings, provided they pay. Call slaves

by another name, legalize their position by a few printed papers, and the traffic becomes a commercial enterprise deserving of every encouragement. A few years ago, while gangs were still being whipped down to the coast in chains, one of the most famous of living African explorers informed the captain of a British gun-boat what was the true state of things upon a Portuguese steamer bound for San Thomé. The captain, full of old-fashioned indignation, proposed to seize the ship. Whereupon the British authorities, flustered at the notion of such impoliteness, reminded him that we were now living in a civilized age. These men and women, who had been driven like cattle over some eight hundred miles of road to Benguela were not to be called slaves. They were "serviçaes," and had signed a contract for so many years, saying they went to San Thomé of their own free will. It was the free will of sheep going to the butcher's. Every one knew that. But the decencies of law and order must be observed.

Within the last two or three years the decencies of law and order have been observed in Benguela with increasing care. There are many reasons for the change. Possibly the polite representations of the British Foreign Office may have had some effect; for England, besides being Portugal's "old ally," is one of the best customers for San Thomé cocoa, and it might upset commercial relations if the cocoa-

drinkers of England realized that they were enjoying their luxury, or exercising their virtue, at the
price of slave labor. Something may also be due
to the presence of the English engineers and mining
prospectors connected with the Robert Williams
Concession. But I attribute the change chiefly to
the helpless little rising of the natives, known as the
"Bailundu war" of 1902. Bailundu is a district
on the route between Benguela and Bihé, and the
rising, though attributed to many absurd causes by
the Portuguese—especially to the political intrigues
of the half-dozen American missionaries in the district—was undoubtedly due to the injustice, violence, and lust of certain traders and administrators.
The rising itself was an absolute failure. Terrified
as the Portuguese were, the natives were more terrified still. I have seen a place where over four
hundred native men, women, and children were
massacred in the rocks and holes where their bones
still lie, while the Portuguese lost only three men.
But the disturbance may have served to draw the
attention of Portugal to the native grievances. At
any rate, it was about the same time that two of
the officers at an important fort were condemned
to long terms of imprisonment and exile for open
slave - dealing, and Captain Amorim, a Portuguese
gunner, was sent out as a kind of special commissioner to make inquiries. He showed real zeal
in putting down the slave - trade, and set a large

number of slaves at liberty with special "letters of freedom," signed by himself — most of which have since been torn up by the owners. His stay was, unhappily, short, but he returned home, honored by the hatred of the Portuguese traders and officials in the country, who did their best to poison him, as their custom is. His action and reports were, I think, the chief cause of Portugal's "uneasiness."

So the horror of the thing has been driven under the surface; and what is worse, it has been legalized. Whether it is diminished by secrecy and the forms of law, I shall be able to judge better in a few months' time. I found no open slave-market existing in Benguela, such as reports in Europe would lead one to expect. The spacious court-yards or compounds round the trading-houses are no longer crowded with gangs of slaves in shackles, and though they are still used for housing the slaves before their final export, the whole thing is done quietly, and without open brutality, which is, after all, unprofitable as well as inhuman.

In the main street there is a government office where the official representative of the "Central Committee of Labor and Emigration for the Islands" (having its headquarters in Lisbon) sits in state, and under due forms of law receives the natives, who enter one door as slaves and go out of another as "serviçaes." Everything is correct. The native, who has usually been torn from his home far in the interior, perhaps as much as eight hundred miles away, and already sold twice, is asked by an interpreter if it is his wish to go to San Thomé, or to undertake some other form of service to a new master. Of course he answers, "Yes." It is quite unnecessary to suppose, as most people suppose, that the interpreter always asks such questions as, "Do you like fish?" or, "Will you have a drink?" though one of the best scholars in the languages of the interior has himself heard those questions asked at an official inspection of "serviçaes" on board ship. It would be unnecessary for the interpreter to invent such questions. If he asked, "Is it your wish to go to hell?" the "serviçal" would say "yes" just the same. In fact, throughout this part of Africa, the name of San Thomé is becoming identical with hell, and when a man has been brought hundreds of miles from his home by an unknown road, and through long tracts of "hungry country" —when also he knows that if he did get back he would probably be sold again or killed—what else can he answer but "yes"? Under similiar circumstances the Archbishop of Canterbury would answer the same.

The "serviçal" says "yes," and so sanctions the contract for his labor. The decencies of law and order are respected. The government of the colony receives its export duty—one of the queerest meth-

ods of "protecting home industries" ever invented.
All is regular and legalized. A series of new rules
for the serviçal's comfort and happiness during his
stay in the islands was issued in 1903, though its
stipulations have not been carried out. And off
goes the man to his death in San Thomé or Il Principe as surely as if he had signed his own death-
warrant. To be sure, there are regulations for his
return. By law, three-fifths of his so-called monthly wages are to be set aside for a "Repatriation
Fund," and in consideration of this he is granted a
"free passage" back to the coast. A more ingenious
trick for reducing the price of labor has never been
invented, but, for very shame, the Repatriation
Fund has ceased to exist, if it ever existed. Ask
any honest man who knows the country well. Ask
any Scottish engineer upon the Portuguese steamers
that convey the "serviçaes" to the islands, and he
will tell you they never return. The islands are
their grave.

These are things that every one knows, but I will
not dwell upon them yet or even count them as
proved, for I have still far to go and much to see.
Leaving the export trade in "contracted labor," I
will now speak of what I have actually seen and
known of slavery on the mainland under the white
people themselves. I have heard the slaves in
Angola estimated at five-sixths of the population
by an Englishman who has held various influential

positions in the country for nearly twenty years. The estimate is only guesswork, for the Portuguese are not strong in statistics, especially in statistics of slavery. But including the very large number of natives who, by purchase or birth, are the family slaves of the village chiefs and other fairly prosperous natives, we might probably reckon at least half the population as living under some form of slavery —either in family slavery to natives, or general slavery to white men, or in plantation slavery (under which head I include the export trade). I have referred to the family slavery among the natives. Till lately it has been universal in Africa, and it still exists in nearly all parts. But though it is constantly pleaded as their excuse by white slave-owners, it is not so shameful a thing as the slavery organized by the whites, if only because whites do at least boast themselves to be a higher race than natives, with higher standards of life and manners. From what I have seen of African life, both in the south and west, I am not sure that the boast is justified, but at all events it is made, and for that reason white men are precluded from sheltering themselves behind the excuse of native customs.

On the same steamer by which I reached Benguela there were five little native boys, conspicuous in striped jerseys, and running about the ship like rats. I suppose they were about ten to twelve years old, perhaps less. I do not know where they came from, but it must have been from some fairly distant part of the interior, for, like all natives who see stairs for the first time, they went up and down them on their hands and knees. They were travelling with a Portuguese, and within a week of landing at Benguela he had sold them all to other white owners. Their price was fifty milreis apiece (nearly £10). Their owner did rather well, for the boys were small and thin—hardly bigger than another native slave boy who was at the same time given away by one Portuguese friend to another as a New-Year's present. But all through this part of the country I have found the price of human beings ranging rather higher than I expected, and the man who told me the price of the boys had himself been offered one of them at that figure, and was simply passing on the offer to myself.

Perhaps I was led to underestimate prices a little by the statement of a friend in England that at Benguela one could buy a woman for £8 and a girl for £12. He had not been to that part of the coast himself, though for five years he had lived in the Katanga district of the Congo State, from which large numbers of the slaves are drawn. Perhaps he had forgotten to take into account the heavy cost of transport from the interior and the risk of loss by death upon the road. Or perhaps he reckoned by the exceptionally low prices pre-

vailing after the dry season of 1903, when, owing
to a prolonged drought, the famine was severe in
a district near the Kunene in southeast Angola,
and some Portuguese and Boer traders took advantage of the people's hunger to purchase oxen
and children cheap in exchange for mealies. Simi-
larly, in 1904, women were being sold unusually
cheap in a district by the Cuanza, owing to a local
famine. Livingstone, in his *First Expedition to
Africa*, said he had never known cases of parents
selling children into slavery, but Mr. F. S. Arnot,
in his edition of the book, has shown that such
things occur (though as a rule a child is sold by
his maternal uncle), and I have myself heard of
several instances in the last few weeks, both for
debt and hunger. Necessity is the slave-trader's
opportunity, and under such conditions the market
quotations for human beings fall, in accordance
with the universal economics.

The value of a slave, man or woman, when landed
at San Thomé, is about £30, but, as nearly as I
could estimate, the average price of a grown man
in Benguela is £20 (one hundred dollars). At that
price the traders there would be willing to supply a large number. An Englishman whom I met
there had been offered a gang of slaves, consisting of forty men and women, at the rate of £18
a head. But the slaves were up in Bihé, and the
cost of transport down to the coast goes for some-

thing; and perhaps there was "a reduction on taking a quantity." However, when he was in Bihé, he had bought two of them from the Portuguese trader at that rate. They were both men. He had also bought two boys farther in the interior, but I do not know at what price. One of them had been with the Batatele cannibals, who form the chief part of the "Révoltés," or rebels, against the atrocious government of the Belgians on the Upper Congo. Perhaps the boy himself really belonged to the race which had sold him to the Bihéan traders. At all events, the racial mark was cut in his ears, and the other "boys" in the Englishman's service were never tired of chaffing him upon his past habits. Every night they would ask him how many men he had eaten that day. But a point was added to the laugh because the ex-cannibal was now acting as cook to the party. Under their new service all these slaves received their freedom.

The price of women on the mainland is more variable, for, as in civilized countries, it depends almost entirely on their beauty and reputation. Even on the Benguela coast I think plenty of women could be procured for agricultural, domestic, and other work at £15 a head or even less. But for the purposes for which women are often bought the price naturally rises, and it depends upon the ordinary causes which regulate such traffic. A full-grown and fairly nice-looking woman may be bought from a trader for £18, but for a mature girl a man must pay more. At least a stranger who is not connected with the trade has to pay more. While I was in the town a girl was sold to a prospector, who wanted her as his concubine during a journey into the interior. Her owner was an elderly Portuguese official of some standing. I do not know how he had obtained her, but she was not born in his household of slaves, for he had only recently come to the country. Most likely he had bought her as a speculation, or to serve as his concubine if he felt inclined to take her. The price finally arranged between him and the prospector for the possession of the girl was one hundred and twenty-five milreis, which was then nearly equal to £25. For the visit of the King of Portugal to England and the revival of the "old alliance" had just raised the value of the Portuguese coinage.

When the bargain was concluded, the girl was led to her new master's room and became his possession. During his journey into the interior she rode upon his wagon. I saw them often on the way, and was told the story of the purchase by the prospector himself. He did not complain of the price, though men who were better acquainted with the uses of the woman-market considered it unnecessarily high. But it is really impossible to fix an average standard of value where such things as beauty and desire are concerned. The purchaser was satisfied, the seller was satisfied. So who was to complain? The girl was not consulted, nor did the question of her price concern her in the least.

I was glad to find that the Portuguese official who had parted with her on these satisfactory terms was no merely selfish speculator in the human market, as so many traders are, but had considered the question philosophically, and had come to the conclusion that slavery was much to a slave's advantage. The slave, he said, had opportunities of coming into contact with a higher civilization than his own. He was much better off than in his native village. His food was regular, his work was not excessive, and, if he chose, he might become a Christian. Being an article of value, it was likely that he would be well treated. "Indeed," he continued, in an outburst of philanthropic emotion, "both in our own service and at San Thomé, the slave enjoys a comfort and well-being which would have been forever beyond his reach if he had not become a slave!" In many cases, he asserted, the slave owed his very life to slavery, for some of the slaves brought from the interior were prisoners of war, and would have been executed but for the profitable market ready to receive them. As he spoke, the old gentleman's face glowed with noble enthusiasm, and I could not but envy him his connection with an institution that was at the same time so salutary to mankind and so lucrative to himself.

As to the slave's happiness on the islands, I cannot yet describe it, but according to the reports of residents, ships' officers, and the natives themselves, it is brief, however great. What sort of happiness is enjoyed on the Portuguese plantations of Angola itself I have already described. As to the comfort and joy of ordinary slavery under white men, with all its advantages of civilization and religion, the beneficence of the institution is somewhat dimmed by a few such things as I have seen, or have heard from men whom I could trust as fully as my own eyes. At five o'clock one afternoon I saw two slaves carrying fish through an open square at Benguela, and enjoying their contact with civilization in the form of another native, who was driving them along like oxen with a sjambok. The same man who was offered the forty slaves at £18 a head had in sheer pity bought a little girl from a Portuguese lady last autumn, and he found her back scored all over with the cut of the *chicote*, just like the back of a trek-ox under training. An Englishman coming down from the interior last African winter, was roused at night by loud cries in a Portuguese trading-house at Mashiko. In the morning he found that a slave had been flogged, and tied to a tree in the cold all night. He was a man who had only lately lost his liberty, and was undergoing the

55

process which the Portuguese call "taming," as applied to new slaves who are sullen and show no pleasure in the advantages of their position. In another case, only a few weeks ago, an American saw a woman with a full load on her head and a baby on her back passing the house where he happened to be staying. A big native, the slave of a Portuguese trader in the neighborhood, was dragging her along with a rope, and beating her with a whip as she went. The American brought the woman into the house and kept her there. Next day the Portuguese owners came in fury with forty of his slaves, breathing out slaughters, but, as is usual with the Portuguese, he shrank up when he was faced with courage. The American refused to give the woman back, and ultimately she was restored to her own distant village, where she still is.

I would willingly give the names in the last case and in all others; but one of the chief difficulties of the whole subject is that it is impossible to give names without exposing people out here to the hostility and persecution of the Portuguese authorities and traders. In most instances, also, not only the people themselves, but all the natives associated with them, would suffer, and the various kinds of work in which they are engaged would come to an end. It is the same fear which keeps the missionaries silent. The Catholic missions are supported by the state. The other missions exist on sufferance. How can missionaries of either division risk the things they have most at heart by speaking out upon a dangerous question? They are silent, though their conscience is uneasy, unless custom puts it to sleep.

Custom puts us all to sleep. Every one in Angola is so accustomed to slavery as part of the country's arrangements that hardly anybody considers it strange. It is regarded either as a wholesome necessity or as a necessary evil. When any question arises upon the subject, all the antiquated arguments in favor of slavery are trotted out again. We are told that but for slavery the country would remain savage and undeveloped; that some form of compulsion is needed for the native's good; that in reality he enjoys more freedom and comfort as a slave than in his free village. Let us at once sweep away all the talk about the native's good. It is on a level with the cant which said the British fought the Boers and brought the Chinese to the Transvaal in order to extend to both races a higher form of religion. The only motive for slavery is money-making, and the only argument in its favor is that it pays. That is the root of the matter, and as long as we stick to that we shall, at least, be saved from humbug.

As to the excuse that there is a difference between slavery and "contracted labor," this is no more than legal cant, just as the other pleas are philanthropic or religious cant. Except in the eyes of the law, it makes no difference whether a man is a "serviçal" or a slave; it makes no difference whether a written contract exists or not. I do not know whether the girl I mentioned had signed a contract expressing her willingness to serve as the prospector's con- cubine for five years, after which she was to be free unless the contract were renewed. But I do know that whether she signed the contract or not, her price and position would have been exactly the same, and that before the five years are up she will in all probability have been sold two or three times over, at diminishing prices. The "serviçal" system is only a dodge to delude the antislavery people, who were at one time strong in Great Britain, and have lately shown signs of life in Portugal. Except in the eyes of a law which is hardly ever enforced, slavery exists almost unchecked. Slaves work the plantations, slaves serve the traders, slaves do the housework of families. Ordinary free wage-earners exist in the towns and among the carriers, but, as a rule, throughout the country the system of labor is founded on slavery, and very few of the Portuguese or foreign residents in Angola would hesitate to admit it.

From Benguela I determined to strike into a dis- trict which has long had an evil reputation as the base of the slave-trade with the interior—a little known and almost uninhabited country.

IV

ON ROUTE TO THE SLAVE CENTRE

HE who goes to Africa leaves time behind. Next week is the same as to-morrow, and it is indifferent whether a journey takes a fortnight or two months. That is why the ox-wagon suits the land so well. Mount an ox-wagon and you forget all time. Like the to-morrows of life, it creeps in its petty pace, and soon after its wheels have reached their extreme velocity of three miles an hour you learn how vain are all calculations of pace and years. Yet, except in the matter of speed, which does not count in Africa, the ox-wagon has most of the qualities of an express-train, besides others of greater value. Its course is at least equally adventurous, and it affords a variety of sensations and experiences quite unknown to the ordinary railway passenger.

Let me take an instance from the recent journey on which I have crossed some four hundred and fifty or five hundred miles of country in two months. A good train would have traversed the distance in a winter's night, and have left only a tedious blank upon the mind. On a railway what should I have known of a certain steep descent which we approached one silent evening after rain? The red surface was just slippery with the wet. The oxen were going quietly along, when, all of a sudden, they were startled by the heavy thud of the wheels jolting over a tree stump on the track. Within a few yards of the brink they set off at a trot, the long and heavy chain hanging loose between them.

"Kouta! Kouta ninni!" ("Brake! Hard on!") shouted the driver, and we felt the Ovampo boy behind the wagon whirl the screw round till the hind wheels were locked. But it was too late. We were over the edge already. Backing and slipping and pulling every way, striking with their horns, charging one another helplessly from behind, the oxen swept down the steep. Behind them, like a big gun got loose, came the wagon, swaying from side to side, leaping over the rocks, plunging into the holes, at every moment threatening to crush the hinder oxen of the span. Then it began to slide sideways. It was almost at right angles to the track. In another second it would turn clean over, with all four wheels in air, or would dash us into a great tree that stood only a few yards down.

"Kouta loula!" ("Loose the brake!") yelled the driver, but nothing could stop the sliding now. We clung on and thought of nothing. Men on the edge of death think of nothing. Suddenly the near hind wheel was thrown against a high ridge of clay. The wagon swung straight, and we were plunged into a river among the struggling oxen, all huddled together and entangled in the chain.

"That was rather rapid," I said, as the wagon came to a dead stop in the mud and we took to the water, but in no language could I translate the expression of the driver's emotions.

Only last wet season the owner of a wagon started down a place like that with twenty-four fine oxen, and at the bottom he had eight oxen, and more beef than he could salt.

Beside another hill lies the fresh grave of a poor young Boer, who was thrown under his wagon wheels and never out-spanned again. Such are the interests of an ox-wagon when it takes to speed.

Or what traveller by train could have enjoyed such experiences as were mine in crossing the Kukema—a river that forms a boundary of Bihé? At that point it was hardly more than five feet deep and twenty yards wide. In a train one would have leaped over it without pause or notice. But in a wagon the passage gave us a whole long day crammed with varied labor and learning. Leading the oxen down to the brink at dawn, we out-spanned and emptied the wagon of all the loads. Then we lifted its "bed" bodily off the four wheels, and spreading the "sail," or canvas hood, under it, we launched it with immense effort into the water as a raft. We anchored it firmly to both banks by the oxen's "reems" (I do not know how the Boers spell those strips of hide, the one thing, except patience, necessary in African travel), and dragging it to and fro through the water, we got the loads over dry in about four journeys. Then the oxen were swum across, and tying some of them to the long chain on the farther side, we drew the wheels and the rest of the wagon under water into the shallows. Next came the task of taking off the "sail" in the water and floating the "bed" into its place upon the beam again—a lifelong lesson in applied hydraulics. When at last the sun set and white man and black emerged naked, muddy, and exhausted from the water, while the wagon itself wallowed triumphantly up the bank, I think all felt they had not lived in vain. Though, to be sure, it was wet sleeping that night, and the rain came sousing down as if poured out of one immeasurable slop-pail.

A railway bridge? What a dull and uninstructive substitute that would have been!

Or consider the ox, how full of personality he is compared to the locomotive! Outwardly he is far from emotional. You cannot coax him as you coax a horse or a dog. A fairly tame ox will allow you to clap his hind quarters, but the only real pleasure you can give him is a lick of salt. For salt even a wild ox will almost submit to be petted. The smell of the salt-bag is enough to keep the whole span sniffing and lowing round the wagon instead of going to feed, and, especially on the "sour veldt," the Sunday treat of salt spread along a rock is a festival of luxury.

But unexpressive as oxen are, one soon learns the inner character of each. There is the wise and willing ox, who will stick to the track and always push his best. He is put at the head of the span. In the middle comes the wild ox, who wants to go any way but the right; the sullen ox, who needs the lash; and the well-behaved representative of gentility, who will do anything and suffer anything rather than work. Nearest the wagon, if possible for as many as four spans, you must put the strong and well-trained oxen, who answer quickly to their names. On them depends the steering and safety of the wagon. At the sound of his name each ox is trained to push his side of the yoke forward, and round trees or corners the wagon follows the curve of safety.

"Blaawberg! Shellback! Rachop! Blomveldt!" you cry. The oxen on the left of the four last spans push forward the ends of their yokes, and edging off to the right, the wagon moves round the segment of an arc. To drive a wagon is like coxing an eight without a rudder.

But on a long and hungry trek even the leaders will sometimes turn aside into the bush for tempting grass, or as a hint that it is time to stop. In a mo-

ment there is the wildest confusion. The oxen behind are dragged among the trees. The chain gets
entangled; two oxen pull on different sides of a
standing trunk; yoke-pegs crack; necks are throttled
by the halters; the wagon is dashed against a solid
stump, and trees and stump and all have to be hewn
down with the axe before the span is free again.
Sometimes the excited and confused animals drag
at the chain while one ox is being helplessly crushed
against a tree. Often a horn is broken off. I know
nothing that suggests greater pain than the crack
of a horn as it is torn from the skull. The ox falls
silently on his knees. Blood streams down his face.
The other oxen go on dragging at the chain. When
released from the yoke, he rushes helplessly over
the bush, trying to hide himself. But flinging him
on his side and tying his legs together, the natives
bind up the horn, if it has not actually dropped,
with a plaster of a poisonous herb they call "mool-
ecky," to keep the blow-flies away. Sometimes it
grows on again. Sometimes it remains loose and
flops about. But, as a rule, it has to be cut off in
the end.

To avoid such things most transport-riders set
a boy to walk in front of the oxen as "toe-leader,"
though it is a confession of weakness. Another
difficulty in driving the ox is his peculiar horror of
mud from the moment that he is in-spanned. By
nature he loves mud next best to food and drink.

He will wallow in mud all a tropical day, and the more slimy it is, the better he likes it. But put him in the yoke, and he becomes as cautious of mud as a cat, as dainty of his feet as a lady crossing Regent Street. It seems strange at first, but he has his reasons. When he comes to one of those ghastly mud-pits ("slaughter-holes" the Boers call them), which abound along the road in the wet season, his first instinct is to plunge into it; but reflection tells him that he has not time to explore its cool depths and delightful stickiness, and that if he falls or sticks the team behind and perhaps the wagon itself will be upon him. So he struggles all he can to skirt delicately round it, and if he is one of the steering oxen, the effort brings disaster either on the wagon or himself. No less terrible is his fate when for hour after hour the wagon has to plough its way through one of the upland bogs; when the wheels are sunk to the hubs, and the legs of all the oxen disappear, and the shrieking whips and yelling drivers are never for a moment still. Why the ox also very strongly objects to getting his tail wet I have not found out.

Another peculiarity is that the ox is too delicate to work if it is raining. Cut his hide to ribbons with rhinoceros whips, rot off his tail with inoculation for lung-sickness, let ticks suck at him till they swell as large as cherries with his blood—he bears all patiently. But if a soft shower descends on him while he is in the yoke, he will work no more. Within a minute or two he gets the sore hump—a terrible thing to have. There is nothing to do but to stop. The hump must be soothed down with wagon-grease—a mixture of soft-soap, black-lead, and tar—and I have heard of wagons halted for weeks together because the owner drove his oxen through a storm. Seeing that it rains in waterspouts nearly every morning or afternoon from October to May, the working-hours are considerably shortened, and unhappy is the man who is in haste. I was in haste.

To be happy in Africa a man should have something oxlike in his nature. Like an ox, or like "him that believeth," he must never make haste. He must accept his destiny and plod upon his way. He must forget emotion and think no more of pleasures. He must let time run over him, and hope for nothing greater than a lick of salt.

But there is one kind of ox which develops further characteristics, and that is the riding-ox. He is the horse of Angola and of all Central Africa where he can live. With ring in nose and saddle on back, he will carry you at a swinging walk over the country, even through marshes where a horse or a donkey would sink and shudder and groan. One of my wagon team was a riding-ox, and it took four men to catch and saddle him. To avoid the dulness of duty he would gallop like a racer and leap like a deer. But when once saddled his ordinary gait was discreet and solemn; and though his name was Buller, I called him "Old Ford," because he somehow reminded me of the Chelsea 'bus.

All the oxen in the team, except Buller, were called by Boer names. Nor was this simply because Dutch is the natural language of oxen. Very nearly every one concerned with wagons in Angola is a Boer, and it is to Boers that the Portuguese owe the only two wagon tracks that count in the country—the road from Benguela through Caconda to Bihé and on towards the interior, and the road up from Mossamedes, which joins the other at Caconda. I think these tracks form the northernmost limit of the trek-ox in Africa, and his presence is entirely due to a party of Boers who left the Transvaal rather more than twenty years ago, driven partly by some religious or political difference, but chiefly by the wandering spirit of Boers. I have conversed with a man who well remembers that long trek—how they started near Mafeking and crept through Bechuanaland, and skirting the Kalahari Desert, crossed Damaraland, and reached the promised land of Angola at last. They were five years on the way —those indomitable wanderers. Once they stopped to sow and reap their corn. For the rest they lived on the game they shot. Now you find about two hundred families of them scattered up and down through South Angola, chiefly in the Humpata district. They are organized for defence on the old Transvaal lines, and to them the Portuguese must chiefly look to check an irruption of natives, such as the Cunyami are threatening now on the Cunene River.

Yet the Portuguese have taken this very opportunity (February, 1905) for worrying them all about licenses for their rifles, and threatening to disarm them if all the taxes are not paid up in full. At various points I met the leading Boers going up to the fort at Caconda, brooding over their grievances, or squatted on the road, discussing them in their slow, untiring way. On further provocation they swore they would trek away into Barotzeland and put themselves under British protection. They even raised the question whether the late war had not given them the rights of British subjects already. A slouching, unwashed, foggy-minded people they are, a strange mixture of simplicity and cunning, but for knowledge of oxen and wagons and game they have no rivals, and in war I should estimate the value of one Boer family at about ten Portuguese forts. They trade to some extent in slaves, but chiefly they buy them for their own use, and they almost always give them freedom at the time of marriage. Their boy slaves they train with the same rigor as their oxen, but when the training is complete the boy is counted specially valuable on the road.

Distances in Africa are not reckoned by miles, but by treks or by days. And even this method is very variable, for a journey that will take a fortnight in the dry season may very well take three months in the wet. A trek will last about three hours, and the usual thing is two treks a day. I think no one could count on more than twelve miles a day with a loaded wagon, and I doubt if the average is as much as ten. But it is impossible to calculate. The record from Bihé to Benguela by the road is six weeks, but you must not complain if a wagon takes six months, and the journey used to be reckoned at a year, allowing time for shooting food on the way. In a straight line the distance is about two hundred and fifty miles, or, by the wagon road, something over four hundred and fifty, as nearly as I can estimate. But when it takes you two or three days to cross a brook and a fortnight to cross a marsh, distance becomes deceptive.

One thing is very noticeable along that wagon road: from end to end of it hardly a single native is to be seen. After leaving Benguela, till you reach the district of Bihé, you will see only one native village, and that is three miles from the road. Much of the country is fertile. Villages have been plentiful in the past. The road passes through their old fields and gardens. Sometimes the huts are still standing, but all is silent and deserted now. Till this winter there was one village left, close upon

the road, about a day's trek past Caconda. But
when I hoped to buy a few potatoes or peppers there,
I found it abandoned like the rest. Where the road
runs, the natives will not stay. Exposed continually to the greed, the violence, and lust of white men
and their slaves, they cannot live in peace. Their
corn is eaten up, their men are beaten, their women
are ravished. If a Portuguese fort is planted in the
neighborhood, so much the worse. Time after time
I have heard native chiefs and others say that a fort
was the cruelest thing to endure of all. It is not
only the exactions of the Chefe in command himself, though a Chefe who comes for about eighteen
months at most, who depends entirely on inter-
preters, and is anxious to go home much richer than
he came, is not likely to be particular. But it is
the brutality of the handful of soldiers under his
command. The greater part of them are natives
from distant tribes, and they exercise themselves by
plundering and maltreating any villagers within
reach, while the Chefe remains ignorant or indifferent. So it comes that where a road or fort or any
other sign of the white man's presence appears the
natives quit their villages one by one, and steal
away to build new homes beyond the reach of the
common enemy. This is, I suppose, that "White
Man's Burden" of which we have heard so much.
This is "The White Man's Burden," and it is the
black man who takes it up.

To the picturesque traveller who is provided with plenty of tinned things to eat, the solitude of the road may add a charm. For it is far more romantic to hear the voice of lions than the voice of man. But, indeed, to every one the road is of interest from its great variety. Here in a short space are to be seen the leading characteristics of all the southern half of Africa—the hot and dry edging near the shore, the mountain zone, and the great interior plateau of forest or veldt, out of which, I suppose, the mountain zone has been gradually carved, and is still being carved, by the wash and dripping from the central marshes. The three zones have always been fairly distinct in every part of Africa that I have known, from Mozambique round to the mouth of the Congo, though in a few places the mountain zone comes down close to the sea.

From Benguela I had to trek for six days, often taking advantage of the moon to trek at night as well, before I saw a trace of water on the surface of the rivers, and nine days before running water was found, though I was trekking in the middle of the wet season. There are one or two dirty wet places, nauseous with sulphur, but all drinking-water for man or ox must be dug for in the beds of the sand rivers, and sometimes you have to dig twelve feet down before the sand looks damp. It is a beautiful land of bare and rugged hills, deeply scarred by weather, and full of the wild and brilliant

colors—the violet and orange—that bare hills always give. But the oxen plod through it as fast
as possible, really almost hurrying in their eager-
ness for a long, deep drink. Yet the district abounds
in wild animals, not only in elands and other antelopes, which can withdraw from their enemies into
deserts drier than teetotal States and can do without a drink for days together. But there are other
animals as well, such as lions and zebras and buffaloes, which must drink every day or die. Somewhere, not far away, there must be a "continuous
water-supply," as a London County Councillor would
say, and hunters think it may be the Capororo or
Korporal or San Francisco, only eight hours south
of the road, where there is always real water and
abundance of game. A thirsty lion would easily
take his tea there in the afternoon and be back in
plenty of time to watch for his dinner along the
road.

Lions are increasing in number throughout the
district, and, I believe, in all Angola, though they
are still not so common as leopards. Certainly they
watch the road for dinner, and all the way from
Benguela to Bihé you have a good chance of hearing them purring about your wagon any night.
Sometimes, then, you may find a certain satisfaction
in reflecting that you are inside the wagon and that
twenty oxen or more are sleeping around you, tied
to their yokes. An ox is a better meal than a man,

but to men as well as to oxen the lions are becoming more dangerous as the wilder game grows scarcer. A native, from the wagon which crossed the Cuando just after mine, was going down for water in the evening, when a lion sprang on him and split the petroleum-can with his claw. The boy had the sense to beat his cup hard against the tin, and the monarch of the forest was so disgusted at the noise that he withdrew; but few boys are so quick, and many are killed, especially in the mountain zone, about one hundred miles from the coast.

I think it is ten years ago now that one of the Brothers of the Holy Spirit was walking in the mission garden at Caconda in the cool of the evening, meditating vespers or something else divine, when he looked up and saw a great lion in the path. Instead of making for the nearest tree, he had the good sense to fall on his knees, and so he went to death with dignity. And on one of the nights when I was encamped near the convent six lions were prowling round it. Vespers were over, but it was a pleasure to me to reflect how much better prepared for death the Brothers were than I.

It is very rarely that you have the luck to see a lion, even where they abound. They are easily hidden. Especially in a country like this, covered with the tawny mounds and pyramids of the white ant, you may easily pass within a few yards of a whole domestic circle of lions without knowing it.

Nor will they touch an armed white man unless pinched with hunger. Yet, in spite of all travellers' libels, the lion is really the king of beasts, next to man. You have only to look at his eye and his forearm to know it. I need not repeat stories of his strength, but one peculiarity of his was new to me, though perhaps familiar to most people. A great hunter told me that when, with one blow of his paw, a lion has killed an ox, he will fasten on the back of the neck and cling there in a kind of ecstasy for a few seconds, with closed eyes. During that brief interval you can go quite close to him unobserved and shoot him through the brain with impunity.

I found the most frequent spoor of lions in a sand river among the mountains, about a week out from Benguela. The country there is very rich in wild beasts—Cape buffalo, many antelopes, and quagga (or Burchell's zebra, as I believe they ought to be called, but the hunters call them quagga).

I was most pleased, however, to find upon the surface of the sand river the spoor of a large herd of elephants which had passed up it the night before. It was difficult to make out their numbers, for they had thrust their trunks deep into the sand for water, and having found it, they evidently celebrated the occasion with a fairy revel, pouring the water over their backs and tripping it together upon the yellow sands. But when they passed on, it was clear that the cows and calves were on the right, while the big males kept the left, and probably forced the passages through the thickest bush. A big bull elephant's spoor on sand is more like an embossed map of the moon with her mountains and valleys and seas than anything else I can think of. A cow's footprint is the map of a simpler planet. And the calf's is plain, like the impression of a paving-hammer, only slightly oval.

There was no nasty concealment about that family. The path they had made through the forest was like the passage of a storm or the course of a battle. They had broken branches, torn up trees, trampled the grass, and snapped off all the sugary pink flowers of the tall aloes, which they love as much as buns in the Zoo. So to the east they had passed away, open in their goings because they had nothing to fear—nothing but man, and unfortunately they have not yet taken much account of him. The hunters say that they move in a kind of zone or rough circle—from the Upper Zambesi across the Cuando into Angola and the district where they passed me, and so across the Cuanza northward and eastward into the Congo, and round towards Katanga and the sources of the Zambesi again. The hunters are not exactly sure that the same elephants go walking round and round the circle. They do not know. But a prince might very profitably spend ten years in following an elephant family round from point to point of its range—profitably, I mean, compared to his ordinary round of royal occupations.

I must not stay to tell of the birds — the flamingoes that pass down the coast, so high that they look no more than geese; the eagles, vultures, and hawks of many kinds; the parrots, few but brilliant; the metallic starling, of two species at least, both among the most gorgeous of birds; the black-headed crane and the dancing crane whose crest is like Cinderella's fan, full-spread and touched with crimson; the many kinds of hornbill, including the bird who booms all night with joy at approaching rain; the great bustard, which the Boers in their usual slipshod way called the pau or peacock, simply because it is big, just as they call the leopard a tiger and the hyena a wolf. Nor must I tell of the guinea-fowl and francolins, or of the various doves, one of which begins with three soft notes and then runs down a scale of seven minor tones, fit to break a mourner's heart; nor of the aureoles and the familiar bird that pleases his wives by growing his tail so long he can hardly hover over the marshes; nor even of our childhood's friend, the honey-guide, whose cheery twitter may lead to the wild bees' nest, but leads just as cheerily to a python or a lion asleep. I cannot speak of these, though I feel there is the making of a horrible tract in that honey-guide.

When you have climbed the mountains—in one

place the wagon crawls over a pass or summit of close upon five thousand feet—you gradually leave the big game (except the lions) and the most brilliant of the birds behind. But the deer become even more plentiful in places. The road is driving them away, as it has driven the natives, and for the same reason. But within a few hours of the road you may find them still—the beautiful roan antelope, the still more beautiful koodoo, the bluebock, the lechwe, the hartebeest (and, I believe, the wildebeest, or gnu, as well), the stinking water-buck, the reedbuck, the oribi, and the little duiker, or "diver," called from its way of leaping through the high grass and disappearing after each bound. It is fine to see any deer run, but there can be few things more delightful than to watch the easy grace of a duiker disappearing in the distance after you have missed him.

Caconda is, in every sense, the turning-point of the journey; first, because the road, after running deviously southeast, here turns almost at right angles northeast on its way to Bihé; secondly, because Caconda marks the entire change in the character of the scenery from mountains to the great plateau of forest and marshy glades. And besides, Caconda is almost the one chance you have of seeing human habitations along the whole course of the journey of some four hundred and fifty miles. The large native town has long since disappeared, though you can trace its ruins; but about five miles south of the road is a rather important Portuguese station of half a dozen trading-houses, a church—only in its second year, but already dilapidated—and a fort, with a rampart, ditch, a toy cannon, and a commandant who tries with real gravity to rise above the level of a toy. Certainly his situation is grave. The Cunyami, who ate up the Portuguese force on the Cunene in September of 1904, have sent him a letter saying they mean next to burn him and his fort and the trading-houses too. He has under his command about thirty black soldiers and a white sergeant; and he might just as well have thirty black ninepins and a white feather. He impressed me as about the steadiest Portuguese I had yet seen, but no wonder he looked grave.

He is responsible, further, for the safety of the Catholic mission, which stands close beside the wagon track itself, overlooking a wide prospect of woodland and grass which reminds one of the view over the Weald of Kent from Limpsfield Common or Crockham Hill. The mission has a tin-roofed church, a gate-house, cells for the four Fathers and five Brothers, dormitories for a kind of boarding-school they keep, excellent workshops, a forge, and a large garden, where the variety of plants and fruits shows what the natives might do but for their unalterable belief that every new plant which comes to maturity costs the life of some one in the village.

Though under Portuguese allegiance and drawing money from the state, all the Fathers and Brothers were French or Alsatian. The superior was a blithe and energetic Norman, who probably could tell more about Angola and its wildest tribes than any one living. But to me, caution made him only polite. The Fathers are said to maintain that acrid old distinction between Catholic and Protestant—not, one would have thought, a matter of great importance— and in the past they have shown much hostility to all other means of enlightening the natives except their own. But things are quieter just now, and over the whole mission itself broods that sense of beauty and calm which seems almost peculiar to Catholicism. One felt it in the gateway with its bell, in the rooms, whitewashed and unadorned, in the banana-walk through the garden, in the work- shops, and even under that hideous tin roof, when some eighty native men and women knelt on the bare, earthen floor during the Mass at dawn.

It is said, but I do not know with what truth, that the Fathers buy from the slave-traders all the "boys" whom they bring up in the mission. The Fathers themselves steadily avoided the subject in conversing with me, but I think it is very probable. About half a mile off is a Sisters' mission, where a number of girls are trained in the same way. When the boys and girls intermarry, as they generally do, they are settled out in villages within sight of the

79

mission. I counted five or six such villages, and this seems to show, though it does not prove, that most of the boys and girls came originally from a distance, or have no homes to return to. On the whole, I am inclined to believe that but for slavery the mission's work must have taken a different form. But why the Fathers should be so cautious about confessing it I do not know, unless they are afraid of being called supporters of the slave-trade because they buy off a few of its victims, and so might be counted among its customers.

From Caconda it took me only three weeks with the wagon to reach the Bihé district, which, I believe, was a record for the wet season. There are five rivers to cross, all of them difficult, and the first and last—the Cuando and the Kukema—dangerous as well. The track also skirts round the marshy source of other great watercourses, and it was with delight that I found myself at the morass which begins the great river Cunene, and, better still, at a little "fairy glen" of ferns and reeds where the Okavango drips into a tiny basin, and dribbles down till it becomes the great river which fills Lake Ngami—Livingstone's Lake Ngami, so far away, on the edge of Khama's country!

The wagon had, besides, to struggle across many of those high, upland bogs which are the terror of the transport-rider in summer-time. The worst and biggest of these is a wide expanse something like an

Irish bog or a wet Salisbury Plain, which the Portuguese call Bourru-Bourru, from the native Vulu-
Vulu. It is over five thousand feet above the sea,
and so bare and dreary that when the natives see
a white man with a great bald head they call it his
Vulu-Vulu. It was almost exactly midsummer
there when I crossed it, and I threw no shadow
at noon, but at night I was glad to cower over a
fire, with all the coats and blankets I had got,
while the mosquitoes howled round me as if for
warmth.

Two points of history I must mention as connected with this part of my journey. The day after
I crossed the Calei I came, while hunting, to a rocky
hill with a splendid view over the valley, only about
a mile from the track. On the top of the hill I found
the remains of ancient stone walls and fortifications
—a big circuit wall of piled stones, an inner circle,
or keep, at the highest point, and many cross-walls
for streets or houses. The whole was just like the
remains of some rude mediæval fortress, and it may
possibly have been very early Portuguese. More
likely, it was a native chief's kraal, though they
build nothing of the kind now. Among the natives
themselves there is a vague tradition of a splendid
ancient city in this region, which they remember as
"The Mountain of Money." Possibly this was the
site, and it is strange that no Boers or other transport-riders I met had ever seen the place.

The other point comes a little farther on—about three days after one crosses the Cunughamba. It is the place by the roadside where, three years ago, the natives burned a Portuguese trader alive and made fetich-medicine of his remains. It happened during the so-called "Bailundu war" of 1902, to which I have referred before. On the spot I still found enough of the poor fellow's bones to make any amount of magic. But if bones were all, I could have gathered far more in the deserted village of Candombo close by. Here a great chief had his kraal, surrounded by ancient trees, and clustered round one of the mightiest natural fortresses I have ever seen. It rises above the trees in great masses and spires of rock, three or four hundred feet high, and in the caves and crevasses of those rocks, now silent and deserted, I found the pitiful skeletons of the men, women, and children of all the little tribe, massacred in the white man's vengeance. Whether the vengeance was just or unjust I cannot now say. I only know that it was exacted to the full.

V

THE AGENTS OF THE SLAVE-TRADE

THE few English people who have ever heard of Bihé at all probably imagine it to themselves as a largish town in Angola famous for its slave-market. Nothing could be less like the reality. There is no town, and there is no slave-market. Bihé is a wide district of forest and marsh, part of the high plateau of interior Africa. It has no mountains and no big rivers, except the Cuanza, which separates it from the land of the Chibokwe on the east. So that the general character of the country is rather indistinctive, and you might as well be in one part of it as another. In whatever place you are, you will see nothing but the broad upland, covered with rather insignificant trees, and worn into quiet slopes by the action of the water, which gathers in morasses of long grass, hidden in the midst of which runs a deep-set stream. Except that it is well watered, fairly cool, and fairly healthy, there is no great attraction in the region. There are a good many leopards and a few wandering lions in the north. Hippos come up the larger

streams to breed, and occasionally you may see a
buck or two. But it is a poor country for beasts
and game, and poor for produce too, though the
orange orchards and strawberry-beds at the mission
stations show it is capable of better things. On the
whole, the impression of the country is a certain
want of character. Often while I have been plod-
ding through woods looking over a grassy valley I
could have imagined myself in Essex, except that
here there are no white roads and no ancient villages. The whole scene is so unlike the popular
idea of tropical Africa that it is startling to meet
a naked savage carrying a javelin, and almost
shocking to meet a lady with only nine inches of
dress.

There is no town and no public slave-market.
The Portuguese fort at Belmonte, once the home of
that remarkable man and redoubtable slave-trader,
Silva Porto, and the scene of his rather splendid
suicide in 1890, may be taken as the centre of the
district. But there are only two or three Portuguese stores gathered round it, and scattered over
the whole country there are only a very limited
number of other trading-houses, the largest being the
headquarters of the Commercial Company of Angola,
established at Caiala, one day's journey from the
fort. The trading-houses are, I think, without exception, worked by slave labor, as are the few plantations of sweet-potato for the manufacture of rum,

which, next to cotton cloth, is the chief coinage in all dealings with the natives. The exchange from the native side consists chiefly of rubber, oxen, and slaves, a load of rubber (say fifty to sixty pounds), an ox, and a young slave counting as about equal in the recognized currency. In English money we might put the value at £9.

It is through these trading-houses that the slave-trade has hitherto been chiefly conducted, and if you want slaves you can buy them readily from any of the larger houses still. But the Bihéans have themselves partly to blame for the ill repute of their country. They are born traders, and will trade in anything. For generations past, probably long before the Portuguese established their present feeble hold upon the country, the Ovimbundu, as they are called, have been sending their caravans of traders far into the interior—far among the tributaries of the Congo, and even up to Tanganyika and the great lakes. Like all traders in Central Africa, they tramp in single file along the narrow and winding foot-paths which are the roads and trade routes of the country. They carry their goods on their heads or shoulders, clamped with shreds of bark between two long sticks, which act as levers. The regulation load is about sixty pounds, but for his own interest a man will sometimes carry double as much. As a rule, they march five or six hours a day, and it takes them about two months to reach the villages of Nanakandundu, which may be taken as the centre of African trade, as it is the central point of the long and marshy watershed which divides the Zambesi from the Congo. For merchandise, they carry with them cotton cloth, beads, and salt, and at present they are bringing out rubber for the most part and a little beeswax. As to slaves, guns, gunpowder, and cartridges are the best exchange for them, owing to the demand for such things among the "Révoltés"—the cannibal and slave-dealing tribes who are holding out against the Belgians among the rivers west of the Katanga district. But the conditions of this caravan slave-trade have been a good deal changed in the last three years, and I shall be able to say more about it after my farther journey into the interior.

As traders, the Bihéans have gained certain advantages. Their Umbundu language almost takes the place in Central West Africa that the Swahili takes on the eastern side. It will carry you fairly well, at all events, along the main foot-paths of trade. They are richer than other tribes, too; they live a little better, they wear rather larger cloths, and get more to eat. But they are naturally despised by neighbors who live by fighting, hunting, fishing, and the manly arts. They are tainted with the softness of trade. In the rising against the Portuguese in 1902, which brought such benefits to all this part of Angola, nearly all of them refused to take any share. They are losing all skill and delight in war. They are almost afraid of their own oxen, and scarcely have the courage to train them. For the wilder side of African life a Bihéan is becoming almost as useless as a board-school boy from Hackney. For skill or sense of beauty in the common arts of metal-work, wood-work, basket-weaving, or ornament, they cannot compare to any of the neighboring tribes. In fact, they are a commercial people, and they pay the full penalty which all commercial peoples have to pay.

Away from the main trade route the country is rather thickly inhabited. The villages lie scattered about in clusters of five or six together. All are strongly stockaded, for custom rather than defence (unless against leopards), and all have rough gates of heavy swinging beams that can be dropped at night, like a portcullis. Most people would say the huts were round; but only the cattle-breeding tribes, like the Ovampos in the south, have round huts. The Bihéan huts are intended to be oblong or square, but as natives have no eye for the straight line, and the roofs are invariably conical, one is easily mistaken. Except to those who have seen nothing better than the filth and grime of English cities, the villages would not appear remarkably clean. They cannot compare for neatness and careful arrangement to the Zulu villages, for instance, nor even to the neighboring Chibokwe. But each family has its separate enclosure, with huts according to its size or the number of the wives, and usually a little patch of garden—for peppers, tomatoes the size of damsons, and perhaps some tobacco. Somewhere in the centre of the enclosures there is sure to be a largish open space with a town hall or public club (onjango). This is much the same in all villages in Central Africa—a pointed, shady roof, supported by upright beams, set far enough apart to admit of entrance on any side. It serves as a parliament-house, a court of justice, a general workshop (especially for metal-workers among the Chibokwe), and for lounge, or place of conversation and agreeable idleness. Perhaps a good club is the best idea we can form of it. It forms a meeting-place for politics, news, chatter, money-making, and games, nor have I ever seen a woman inside.

On the dusty floor a piece of hard ground, three or four inches above the rest of the surface, is usually left as the throne or place of honor for the chief. There he reclines, or sits on a stool six inches high, and exercises the usual royal functions. He is clothed in apparel which one soon comes to recognize as kingly. It is some sort of cap or hat and a shirt. The original owners of both were probably European, but time enough has elapsed to secure them the veneration due to the symbols of established authority, and they are covered with layer upon layer of tradition. Thus arrayed, the chief

88

sits from morning till evening in the very heart of his kingdom and contemplates its existence. Sometimes a criminal case or a dispute about debt comes up for his decision. Then he has the assistance of three elders of the village, and in extreme cases he is supposed to seek the wisdom of the white man at the fort. But the expense of such wisdom is at least equal to its value, and rather than risk the delay, the uncertainty of justice, and the certainty of some contribution to the legal fees in pigs, oxen, or rubber, the villagers usually settle up their own differences more quickly and good-naturedly now than they used, and so out of the strong comes forth sweetness. In the last resort the ancient tests of poison and boiling water are still regarded as final (as, indeed, they are likely to be), and men who have lived long in the country and know it well assure me that those tests are still recommended by the wisdom of the white man at the fort.

Adjoining the public square the chief has his own enclosure, with the royal hut for his wives, who may number anything from four to ten or so, the number, as in all countries, being regulated by the expense. Leaving the politics, law, games, and other occupations of public life to the more strictly intellectual sex, the wives, like the other women of the village, follow the primeval labor of the fields (which, as a rule, are of their own making), and go out at dawn with basket and hoe on their heads and babies wrapped to their backs, returning in the afternoon to pound the meal in wooden mortars, and otherwise prepare the family's food.

I have had difficulty in finding out why one man is chief rather than another. It is not entirely a matter of blood or of wealth, still less of character. But all these go for something, and the villagers themselves appear to have a certain voice in the selection, though the choice must lie within the bounds of the "blood royal." Constitutionally, I believe, the same principle holds in the case of the British crown. I have never heard of a disputed succession in an African village, though disputes often arise in the larger tribes, as among the Cunyami, where a very intelligent chief was lately poisoned by his brother, as too peaceable and philosophic for a king. But there is no longer a king or head chief in Bihé. The last was captured over twenty years ago, after a mythical resistance in his umbala or capital of Ekevango, the ancient trees of which can be seen from the American mission at Kamundongo. So he joined the kings in exile, and, I believe, still drags out an existence of memories in the Santiago of Portuguese Guinea. There remain the chiefs of districts, and the headmen of villages, and though, as I have described, their state is hardly to be distinguished from that of royalty, they are generally allowed to live to enjoy it.

But best of all I like a chief in his moments of

condescension, when he steps down from his four inches of mud and squats in the level dust with the rest, just to show the young men how games should be played. Chiefs appear to be specially good at the games which take the place of cards and similar leisurely pastimes in European courts. The favorite is a mixture of backgammon and "Archer up." It is played either on a hewn log or in the dust, and consists in getting a large number of beans through four rows of holes. At first it looks like "go as you please," but in time, as you watch, certain rules rise out of chaos, and you find that the best player really wins. The best player is nearly always the chief, and I have no doubt he devotes long hours of his magnificent leisure to pondering over the more scientific aspects of the pursuit. In the same way one has heard of European kings renowned for their success at Monte Carlo, baccarat, and bridge.

But, besides the games, the chiefs are the repositories of traditional wisdom, and for this function it is harder to find a parallel among civilized courts. The wisdom is usually expressed in symbolic diagrams upon the dust. In his moments of fatherly instruction the chief will smooth a surface with his hand, and on it trace with his fingers a mystic line— I think it must always be a continuous and unbroken line—which expresses some secret of human existence. Sometimes the design is merely heraldic, as in this conventional figure of a one-headed eagle, which I recommend to the German Emperor for a new flag. But generally there is a hidden significance, not to be detected without superior information. The chief, for instance, will imprint five spots on the sand, and round them trace an interminable line which just misses each spot in turn. The five spots signify the vain ambitions of man, and the line is man's vain effort ever to reach them. Or again, he will mark nine points with his finger on the sand and trace a line which will surround eight of them and always come back to the ninth, which stands in the centre. Till superior wisdom informed you, probably you would hardly guess that the eight points are the "thoughts" of man, and that the ninth, to which the line always returns, is the end of the whole matter—that no solution of the thoughts of man is ever to be found:

"Earth could not answer, nor the seas that mourn."

It is surprising to find a philosophy so Omarian so far from Nashipur and Babylon, but there it is.

The Ovimbundu of Bihé, like all the natives in this part of Africa, have also a large stock of proverbs. Out of a number of Umbundu proverbs I have heard, we may take three as pretty fair samples of wisdom: "If you miss, don't break your bow," which I like better than the English doggerel of, "Try, try, try again," or, "A bad carpenter quarrels with his tools"; "Speak of water and the fish are gone," a proverb that will bear many interpretations, though I think it really means, "Never introduce your donah to your pal"; and, "The lion needs no servant," which I like best of all, but can find no parallel for among a race so naturally snobbish as ourselves. A variation of the proverb runs, "A pig has no servant, a lion needs none." I have heard many stories of folk-lore, too — legends or fables of animals, something in the manner of "Uncle Remus." As that the mole came late and got no tail, or that the hen one day claimed the crocodile for her brother, and all the beasts, under the hippo, assembled to support the crocodile, and all the birds, under the eagle, to support the hen. After long argument the hen demanded whether the crocodile did not spring from an egg like herself. The claim was admitted, and since then the crocodile and the hen have been brother and sister.

More in the character of "Uncle Remus" is the favorite story how the dog became the friend of man. Once upon a time a leopard intrusted a starving dog with the care of her cubs. All went well till a turtle appeared upon the scene and induced the dog to bring out one of the cubs and share it between them, saying she could show the leopard the same cub twice over and persuade her that the whole brood was flourishing. This went on very satisfactorily for some days, the dog and turtle devouring a cub daily, and the dog producing one of the cubs for the leopard's inspection twice, three times, four times over, as the case demanded. At last only one cub was left alive, and it had to be produced eight or nine times, according to the original number of the litter. Next day there was no cub left at all, and the dog invited the leopard to walk into the den and contemplate her healthy young nursery for herself. No sooner had she entered the cave than the dog bolted for the nearest village, and rushed among the huts, crying, "Man, man, the leopard is coming!" Since which day the dog has never left the village, but has remained the friend of man.

Nearly akin to folk-lore are the quaint sayings and brief stories which sum up the daily experience of a people. Take, for instance, this dilemma, turning on an antipathy which appears to be the common heritage of all mankind: "I go to bury my mother-in-law. The king sends for me to attend his council. If I do not go to the king, he will cut my head off. If I do not bury my mother-in-law, she may come to life. I go to bury my mother-in-law." More unusual to English ears was the statement made quite seriously in my presence by a young man who was inquiring about the manner of life in England. "If you can buy things there," he said, "there is no need to marry." Certainly not;

when you can buy meal in a shop, why expose your-self to the annoyance and irritation of keeping wives to sow and gather and pound and sift the mealies for you?

Like all the tribes of this region, the Bihéans are much given to dancing, especially under a waxing moon, and when the dry season is just beginning— say in the end of April. It so happens that the Bihéan dances I have seen have been almost al-ways the dances of children, and they were very pretty. Sometimes a girl is lifted on the hands of a group of children and jumped up and down in that perilous position, while the others dance and sing round her. Sometimes the dance is a kind of "hen and chickens" or "prisoners' base." But the pret-tiest dance I know is the frog dance, in which the children crouch down in rows and leap over the ground, clapping their elbows sharply against their naked sides, with exactly the effect of Spanish cas-tanets, while their hard, bare feet stamp the dust in time. Then they have a game something like "hunt the slipper," two rows sitting on the ground opposite each other, and tossing about a knotted cloth with their legs. All these dances and games are accompanied by monotonous and violent sing-ing, the words of the song being repeated over and over again. They are generally of the simplest kind, and have no apparent connection with the dance. The song which I heard to the frog dance, for instance, ran: "I am going to my mother in the village. I am going to my mother in the village."

Various musical instruments are used all through this part of Africa, perhaps the simplest being the primeval fiddle. A string of bark is stretched across half a gourd, and made to vibrate with a notched stick drawn to and fro across it. The player holds the gourd against his breastbone, and hisses through his teeth in time to the movement, sometimes adding a few words of song. After an hour or so he thus works himself and his audience up almost to hypnotic frenzy. If this is the simplest instrument, the alimba is the most elaborate. It is a series of wooden slats—twelve or fourteen—attached to a curved framework about six feet long. Behind the slats gourds are fixed as sounding-boards, but the number of gourds does not necessarily correspond to the slats. The player squats in the middle of the curve and strikes the wood with rubber hammers. Though there is no true scale of any kind, the individual notes are often fine and the result very beautiful, especially before the singing begins.

But the true instruments of Central Africa are the ochisanji and the drum. The ochisanji is the primeval piano, a row of iron keys (sometimes two rows) being laid upon a small oblong board, which is covered with carving. The keys are played with the thumbs, and some loose beads or bits of iron at the bottom of the board set up a rattling which, to us, does not improve the music. But it is really a beautiful instrument, and I can well imagine that when a native hears it far from his village he is filled with the same yearning that a Swiss feels at the sound of a cow-horn. It is the common accompaniment to all native songs, the words being spoken to it rather than sung. Nearly all carriers have an ochisanji tied round their necks, and one of my carriers used to sing me a minor song, lamenting his poverty, his loss of an ox, and loss of a lover, and between each verse he put in a sobbing refrain, very musical and melancholy. The ochisanji also is sometimes laid across half a hollow gourd, to improve the tone.

And then there is the drum! The drum is undoubtedly as much the national instrument of Africa as the bagpipe is of Scotland. It is made out of almost anything—the bark of a tree stitched together into a cylinder and covered with goat-skin at each end, or a hollow stump, or even a large gourd will serve. But there is one kind of drum valued above all others—so precious that, when a village owns one, it is kept in a little house all to itself. This drum is shaped just like an old-fashioned carpet-bag, half open, except that the top is longer than the bottom. It measures about four feet high by three feet long, and is about eight inches broad at the bottom, the sides tapering as towards the mouth. The inside is hollowed out with axes, the whole being made of one solid block of wood. Half-way along the sides, near the top or mouth, rough lumps of rubber are fixed, and these are thumped either with a rubber-headed drumstick or with the fist, while a second player taps the wood with a bit of stick. The result is the most overwhelming sound I have heard. I know the wardrum, and I know the glory of the drums in the Ninth Symphony, but I have never known an instrument that had such an effect upon the mind as this African ochingufu. To me it is intensely depressing. At its first throb my heart sinks into my boots. Far from being roused to battle by such a sound, my instinct would be to hide under the blanket. But to the native soul it is truly inspiring. To all their great dances this is the sole accompaniment, and for hour after hour of the night they will keep up its unvaried beat without intermission, one drummer after another taking his turn, while the dance goes on, and from time to time the dancers and the crowd raise their monotonous chant. The invention of this terrible instrument was altogether beyond Bihéan art, though they sometimes imitate the models for themselves. But the greater number of the drums are still imported from the far interior, around the sources of the Zambesi, and they have become a regular article of commerce. Many a time, along the great foot-path of trade, I have seen a carrier bringing down the drum as part of his load from some village hundreds of miles east of Bihé, and I have wondered at the demon of terror and revelry which lay enchanted in that common-looking piece of hollow wood.

But then the whole country is full of other demons, not of revelry, but certainly of terror. At the gates (that is, the narrow gaps in the stockade) of nearly all villages stands a little cluster of sticks with the skulls of antelopes on their tops. Sometimes the sticks are roofed over with a little straw. Sometimes they are tied up with strips of cloth like little flags, or a few bits of broken pot are laid in the shrine and a little meal is scattered around. Often a similar shrine is set up inside the village itself, and where a chief lives in his umbala or capital among the ancient trees it will very likely have developed into a "Kandundu"—the abode of a great magic spirit, who dwells in a kind of cage on the top of a long pole. The worship of the Kandundu is in some vague way connected with a frog, and the spirit is supposed to reveal himself and utter his oracles to the witch-doctor in that form. But if you get a chance of exploring that cage on the palm pole, you generally find no frog, but only greasy rags. The bright point about the Kandundu is that the spirit can become actively benevolent instead of being merely a terror to be averted, like most of the spirits in Africa. The same high praise can also be given to Okevenga, whose name may be connected with the great river Okavango, and who is certainly a benevolent spirit, watching over women, and helping them with their fields, their sowing, and their children.

These are the only two exceptions I have hitherto met with to the general malignity of the spiritual world in this part of Africa. The spirits of the dead are always evil disposed, when they return at all, and they are the common agents of the witchcraft that plays so large a part in village life and is the cause of so much slavery. It is not uncommon for a woman to kill herself in order to haunt her mother-in-law or another wife of whom she is jealous. And it is partly to keep the spirit quiet for the year or so before it gradually fades away into nothingness that poles surmounted by the skulls of oxen are set above a grave. Partly also this is to display the wealth of the family, which could afford to kill an ox or two at the funeral feast; just as in England the mass of granite heaped upon a tomb is intended rather to establish the respectability of the deceased than to secure his repose.

Slavery exists quite openly throughout Bihé in the three forms of family slavery among the natives themselves, domestic slavery to the Portuguese traders, and slavery on the plantations. The purchase of slaves is rendered easier by certain native customs, especially by the peculiar law which gives the possession of the children to the wife's brother, even during the lifetime of both parents. The law has many advantages in a polygamous country, and the parents can redeem their children and make them their own property by various payments, but, unless the children are redeemed, the wife's brother can claim them for the payment of his own debts or the debts of his village. I think this is chiefly done in the payment of family debts for witchcraft, and I have seen a case in which, for a debt of that kind, a mother has been driven to pawn her own child herself. Her brother had murdered her eldest boy, and, going into the interior to trade, had died there. Of course his wives and other relations charged her with witchcraft through her murdered boy's spirit, and she was condemned to pay a fine. She had nothing to pay but her two remaining children, and as the girl was married and with child, she was unwilling to take her. So she pawned her little boy to a native for the sum required, though she knew he would almost certainly be sold as a slave to the Portuguese long before she could redeem him, and she would have no chance of redress.

In that particular case, which happened recently, a missionary, who knew the boy, advanced an ox in his place; but the missionary's intervention was, of course, entirely accidental, and the facts are only typical of the kind of thing that is repeatedly happening in places where there is no one to help or to know.

In a village in the northwest of Bihé I have seen

a man—the headman of the place—who has been gradually tempted on by a Portuguese trader till he has sold all his children and all the other relations in his power for rum. Last of all, one morning at the beginning of this winter (1905), he told his wife to smarten herself up and come with him to the trader's house. She appears to have been a particularly excellent woman, of whom he was very fond. Yet when they arrived at the store he received a keg of rum and went home with it, leaving his wife as the trader's property.

In the same district I met a boy who told me how his father was sold in the middle of last January. They were slaves to a native named Onbungululu in the village of Chariwewa, and his father, in company with twenty other of the slaves, was sold to a certain Portuguese trader, who acts on behalf of the "Central Committee of Labor and Emigration," and was draughted quietly away through the bush for the plantations in San Thomé.

To show how low the price of human beings will run, I may mention a case that happened in January, 1905, on the Cuanza, just over the northeast frontier of Bihé. I think I noticed in an earlier chapter that there was much famine there last winter, and so it came about that a woman was sold for forty yards of cloth and a pig (cloth being worth about fourpence a yard), and was brought into Bihé by the triumphant purchaser.

But that was an exception, and the following instance of the slave-trader's ways is more typical. Last summer a Portuguese, who is perhaps the most notorious and reckless slave-trader now living in Bihé, and whose name is familiar far in the interior of Africa, sent a Bihéan into the southern Congo with orders to bring out so many slaves and with chains to bind them. As the Bihéan was returning with the slaves, one of them escaped, and the trader demanded another slave and three loads of rubber as compensation. This the Bihéan has now paid, but in the mean time the trader's personal slaves have attacked and plundered his village. The trader himself is at present away on his usual business in the remote region of the Congo basin called Lunda, and it is thought his return is rather doubtful; for the "Révoltés" and other native tribes in those parts accuse him of selling cartridges that will not fit their rifles. But he appears to have been flourishing till quite lately, for the natives in the village where I am staying say that he has sent out a little gang of seven slaves, which passed down the road only the day before yesterday, on their way to San Thomé.

But about that road, which has been for centuries the main slave route from the interior to the Portuguese coast, I shall say more in my next letter, when I have myself passed up and down it for some hundreds of miles and had an opportunity of seeing its present condition.

VI

THE WORST PART OF THE SLAVE ROUTE

I WAS going east along the main trade route —
the main slave route—by which the Bihéans pass
to and fro in their traffic with the interior. It is
but a continuation of the track from Benguela, on
the coast, through the district of Bihé, and it follows the long watershed of Central Africa in the
same way. The only place where that watershed
is broken is at the passage of the Cuanza, which
rises far south of the bank of high ground, but has
made its way northward through it at a point some
three days' journey east of the Bihéan fort at Belmonte, and so reaches the sea on the west coast, not
very far below Loanda.

It forms the frontier of Bihé, dividing that race
of traders from the primitive and savage tribes of
the interior. But on both sides along its banks and
among its tributaries you find the relics of other
races of very different character from the Bihéans
—the Luimbi, whose women still wear the old coinage of white cowry-shells in their hair, and the
Luchazi, who support their loads with a strap round

their foreheads, like the Swiss, and whose women dress their hair with red mud, and carry their babies straddled round the hip instead of round the back.

Going eastward along this pathway into the interior, I had reached the banks of the Cuanza one evening towards the end of the wet season. It had been raining hard, but at sunset there was a sullen clear which left the country steaming with damp. On my left I could hear the roar of the Cuanza rapids, where the river divides among rocky islands and rushes down in breakers and foam. And far away, across the river's broad valley, I could see the country into which I was going—straight line after line of black forest, with the mist rising in pallid lines between. It was like a dreary skeleton of the earth.

Such was my first sight of "the Hungry Country" —that accursed stretch of land which reaches from just beyond the Cuanza almost to the Portuguese fort at Mashiko. How far that may be in miles I cannot say exactly. A rapid messenger will cover the distance in seven days, but it took me nine, and it takes most people ten or twelve. My carriers had light loads, and in spite of almost continuous fevers and poisoned feet we went fast, walking from six till two or even four o'clock without food, so that, even allowing for delays at the deep morasses and rivers and the long climbs up the forest hills, I think we cannot have averaged less than twenty miles a day, and probably we often made twenty-five. I should say that the distance from the Cuanza to Mashiko must be somewhere about two hundred and fifty miles, and it is Hungry Country nearly the whole way.

Still less is it certain how far the district extends in breadth from north to south. I have often looked from the top of its highest uplands, where a gap in the trees gave me a view, in the hope of seeing something beyond. But, though the hill might be six thousand feet above the sea, I could never get a sight of anything but forest, and still more forest, till the waves of the land ended in a long, straight line of blue—almost as straight and blue as the sea—and nothing but forest all the way, with not a trace of man. Yet the whole country is well watered. Deep and clear streams run down the middle of the open marshes between the hills. For the first day or two of the journey they flow back into the Cuanza basin, but when you have climbed the woody heights beyond, you find them running north into the Kasai, that great tributary of the Congo, and south into the Lungwebungu or the Luena, the tributaries of the Zambesi. At some points you stand at a distance of only two days' journey from the Kasai and the Lungwebungu on either side, and there is water flowing into them all the year round. In Africa it is almost always the want of water that makes a Hungry Country, but here the rule does not hold.

At first I thought the character of the soil was sufficient reason for the desert. Except for the black morasses, it is a loose white sand from end to end. The sand drifts down the hills like snow, and banks itself up along any sheltered or level place, till as you plod through it hour after hour, almost ankle-deep, while your shadow gradually swallows itself up as the sun climbs the sky, your only thought becomes a longing for water and a longing for one small yard of solid ground. The trees are poor and barren, and I noticed that the farther I went the soft joints of the grasses, which ought to be sweet, became more and more bitter, till they tasted like quinine.

This may be the cause of another thing I noticed. All living creatures in this region are crazy for salt, just like oxen on a "sour veldt." Salt is far the best coinage you can take among the Chibokwe. I do not mean our white table-salt. They reject that with scorn, thinking it is sugar or something equally useless; but for the coarse and dirty "bay-salt" they will sell almost anything, and a pinch of it is a greater treat to a child than a whole bride-cake would be in England.

I have tested it especially with the bees that swarm in these forests and produce most of the bees-wax that goes to Europe. I first noticed their love of salt when I salted some water one afternoon in the vain hope of curing the poisoned sores on my feet. In half an hour the swarms of bees had driven me from my tent. I was stung ten times, and had to wait about in the forest till the sun set, when the bees vanished, as by signal.

Another afternoon I tested them by putting a heap of sugar, a paper smeared with condensed milk, and a bag of salt tightly wrapped up in tar-paper side by side on the ground. I gave them twenty minutes, and then I found nothing on the sugar, five flies on the milk, and the tar-paper so densely covered with bees that they overlapped one another as when they swarm. For want of any-thing better, they will fight over a sweaty shirt in the same way; and once, by the banks of a stream, they sent all my carriers howling along the path by creeping up under their loin-cloths. The butter-flies seek salt also. If you spread out a damp rag anywhere in tropical Africa, you will soon have brilliant butterflies on it. But if you add a little salt in the Hungry Country, the rag will be a blaze of colors, unless the bees come and drive the butter-flies off.

As I said, the natives feel the longing too. Among the Chibokwe, the women burn a marsh-grass into a potash powder as a substitute; and if a native squats down in front of you, puts out a long, pink tongue and strokes it appealingly with his finger, you may know it is salt he wants. The scarcity has become worse since the Belgians, following their usual highwayman methods, have robbed the natives of the great salt-pans in the south of the Congo State and made them a trade monopoly.

In the character of the soil, then, there seemed to be sufficient reason for the name of the country, and I should have been satisfied with it but for distinct evidences that a few spots along the path have been inhabited not so very long ago. Here and there you come upon plants which grow generally or only on the site of deserted villages or fields; such as the atundwa—a plant with branching fronds that smell like walnut leaves. It yields a fruit whose hard and crimson case just projects from the ground and holds a gray bag of seeds, very sour, and almost as good to eat or drink as lemons. But still more definite is the evidence of travellers, like the missionary explorer Mr. Arnot, who first traversed the country over twenty years ago, and has described to me the villages he found there then. There was, for instance, the large Chibokwe town of Peho, which was built round the head of a marsh close upon the main path some two or three days west of Mashiko. You will still find the place marked, about the size of London, on any map of Angola or Africa, but I have looked everywhere for it along the route in vain. A Portuguese once told me he thought it was a few days' journey north of his house near

Mashiko. But he was wrong. The whole place has entirely disappeared, and has less right than Nineveh to a name on a modern map.[1]

The Chibokwe have a custom of destroying their villages and abandoning the site whenever a chief dies, and this in itself is naturally very puzzling to all geographers. But I think it hardly explains the utter abandonment of the Hungry Country. It is commonly supposed that no wild animals will live in the region, but that is not true, either. Many times, when I have wandered away from the foot-path, I have put up various antelopes—lechwe and duikers—and beside the marshes in the early morning I have seen the fresh spoor of larger deer, as well as of porcupines and wart-hogs. Cranes are fairly common, and green parrots very abundant. Almost every night one hears the leopards roar. "Roar" is not the word: it is that deep note of pleasurable expectancy that they sound a quarter of an hour before feeding-time at the Zoo, and they would not make that noise if there was nothing in the country to eat. All these reasons put together drive me unwillingly to think there may be some truth in the native belief that the whole land has been laid under a curse which will never be removed. As I write, the rumor reaches us that the basin of the Zambesi and all its tributaries have just been

[1] Commander Cameron describes the town and its chief, Mona Peho, in *Across Africa*, p. 426 (1876).

awarded to Great Britain, so that nearly the whole of the Hungry Country will come under English rule. It is important for England, therefore, that the curse should be forgotten, and in time it may be. All I know for certain is that undoubtedly a curse lies upon the country now.[1]

There are two ferries over the Cuanza, one close under the Portuguese fort, the other a comfortable distance up-stream, well out of observation. It is a typically Portuguese arrangement. The Commandant's duty is to stop the slave-trade, but how can he be expected to see what is going on a mile or so away! Even as you come down to the river, you find slave-shackles hanging on the bushes. You cross the stream in dugout canoes, running the chance of being upset by one of the hippos which snort and pant a little farther up. You enter the forest again, and now the shackles are thick upon the trees. This is the place where most of the slaves, being driven down from the interior, are untied. It is safe to let them loose here. The Cuanza is just in front, and behind them lies the long stretch of Hungry Country, which they could never get through alive if they tried to run back to their homes. So it is that the trees on the western

[1] The King of Italy's award on the disputed frontier between British Barotzeland and Portuguese Angola was not published, in fact, till July, 1905. Great Britain received only part of her claim, and the Hungry Country, together with the whole of the slave route, remains under Portuguese misgovernment.

edge of the Hungry Country bear shackles in pro-
fusion—shackles for the hands, shackles for the feet,
shackles for three or four slaves who are clamped
together at night. The drivers hang them up with
the idea of using them again when they return for
the next consignment of human merchandise; but,
as a rule, I think, they find it easier to make new
shackles as they are wanted.

A shackle is easily made. A native hacks out an
oblong hole in a log of wood with an axe; it must
be big enough for two hands or two feet to pass
through, and then a wooden pin is driven through
the hole from side to side, so that the hands or feet
cannot stir until it is drawn out again. The two
hands or feet do not necessarily belong to the same
person. You find shackles of various ages—some
quite new, with the marks of the axe fresh upon
them, some old and half eaten by ants. But none
can be very old, for in Africa all dead wood quickly
disappears, and this is a proof that the slave-trade
did not really end after the war of 1902, as easy-
going officials are fond of assuring us.

When I speak of the shackles beside the Cuanza,
I do not mean that this is the only place where they
are to be found. You will see them scattered along
the whole length of the Hungry Country; in fact,
I think they are thickest at about the fifth day's
journey. They generally hang on low bushes of
quite recent growth, and are most frequent by

the edge of the marshes. I cannot say why. There
seems to be no reason in their distribution. I have
been assured that each shackle represents the death
of a slave, and, indeed, one often finds the remains
of a skeleton beside a shackle. But the shackles are
so numerous that if the slaves died at that rate even
slave-trading would hardly pay, in spite of the immense profit on every man or woman who is brought
safely through. It may often happen that a sick
slave drags himself to the water and dies there. It
may be that some drivers think they can do without
the shackles after four or five days of the Hungry
Country. But at present I can find no satisfactory
explanation of the strange manner in which the
shackles are scattered up and down the path. I
only know that between the Cuanza and Mashiko
I saw several hundreds of them, and yet I could not
look about much, but had to watch the narrow and
winding foot-path close in front of me, as one always
must in Central Africa.

That path is strewn with dead men's bones. You
see the white thigh-bones lying in front of your feet,
and at one side, among the undergrowth, you find
the skull. These are the skeletons of slaves who
have been unable to keep up with the march, and
so were murdered or left to die. Of course the ordinary carriers and travellers die too. It is very
horrible to see a man beginning to break down in
the middle of the Hungry Country. He must go on

or die. The caravan cannot wait for him, for it has
food for only the limited number of days. I knew
a distressful Irishman who entered the route with
hardly any provision, broke down in the middle,
and was driven along by his two carriers, who
threatened his neck with their axes whenever he
stopped, and only by that means succeeded in getting him through alive. Still worse was a case
among my own carriers—a little boy who had been
brought to carry his father's food, as is the custom.
He became crumpled up with rheumatism, and I
found he had bad heart-disease as well. He kept
on lying down in the path and refusing to go farther.
Then he would creep away into the bush and hide
himself to die. We had to track him out, and his
father beat him along the march till the blood ran
down his back.

But with slaves less trouble is taken. After a
certain amount of beating and prodding, they are
killed or left to die. Carriers are always buried by
their comrades. You pass many of their graves,
hung with strips of rag or decorated with a broken
gourd. But slaves are never buried, and that is
an evidence that the bones on the path are the bones
of slaves. The Bihéans have a sentiment against
burying slaves. They call it burying money. It
is something like their strong objections to burying
debtors. The man who buries a debtor becomes
responsible for the debts; so the body is hung up

on a bush outside the village, and the jackals consume it, being responsible for nothing.

Before the great change made by the "Bailundu war" of 1902, the horrors of the Hungry Country were undoubtedly worse than they are now. I have known Englishmen who passed through it four years ago and found slaves tied to the trees, with their veins cut so that they might die slowly, or laid beside the path with their hands and feet hewn off, or strung up on scaffolds with fires lighted beneath them. My carriers tell me that this last method of encouraging the others is still practised away from the pathway, but I never saw it done myself. I never saw distinct evidence of torture. The horrors of the road have certainly become less in the last three years, since the rebellion of 1902. Rebellion is always good. It always implies an unendurable wrong. It is the only shock that ever stirs the self-complacency of officials.

I have not seen torture in the Hungry Country. I have only seen murder. Every bone scattered along that terrible foot-path from Mashiko to the Cuanza is the bone of a murdered man. The man may not have been killed by violence, though in most cases the sharp-cut hole in the skull shows where the fatal stroke was given. But if he was not killed by violence, he was taken from his home and sold, either for the buyer's use, or to sell again to a Bihéan, to a Portuguese trader, or to the agents

who superintend the "contract labor" for San
Thomé, and are so useful in supplying the cocoa-
drinkers of England and America, as well as in en-
riching the plantation-owners and the government.
The Portuguese and such English people as love to
stand well with Portuguese authority tell us that
most of the men now sold as slaves are criminals,
and so it does not matter. Very well, then; let us
make a lucrative clearance of our own prisons by
selling the prisoners to our mill-owners as factory-
hands. We might even go beyond our prisons. It
is easy to prove a crime against a man when you
can get £10 or £20 by selling him. And if each of
us that has committed a crime may be sold, who
shall escape the shackles?

The most recent case of murder that I saw was
on my return through the Hungry Country, the
sixth day out from Mashiko. The murdered man
was lying about ten yards from the path hidden in
deep grass and bracken. But for the smell I should
have passed the place without noticing him as I
have no doubt passed scores, and perhaps hundreds,
of other skeletons that lie hidden in that forest.
How long the man had been murdered I could not
say, for decay in Africa varies with the weather, but
the ants generally contrive that it shall be quick. I
think the thing must have been done since I passed
the place on my way into the country, about a
month before. But possibly it was a few days

earlier. My "headman" had heard of the event (a native hears everything), but it did not impress him or the other carriers in the least. It was far too common. Unhappily I do not understand enough Umbundu to make out the exact date or the details, except that the man was a slave who broke down with the usual shivering fever on the road and was killed with an axe because he could go no farther. As to the cause of death there was no doubt. When I tried to raise the head, the thick, woolly hair came off in my hand like a woven pad, leaving the skull bare, and revealing the deep gash made by the axe at the base of the skull just before it merges with the neck. As I set it down again, the skull broke off from the backbone and fell to one side. Having laid a little earth upon the body, I went on. It would take an army of sextons to bury all the poor bones which consecrate that path.

Yet, in spite of the shackles hanging on the trees, and in spite of the skeletons upon the path and the bodies of recently murdered men, I have not seen a slave caravan such as has been described to me by almost every traveller who has passed along that route into the interior. I mean, I have not seen a gang of slaves chained together, their hands shackled, and their necks held fast in forked sticks. I am not sure of the reason; there were probably many reasons combined. It is just the end of the wet season, just the time when the traders think of send-

ing in for slaves, and not of bringing them out.
Directly the natives in the Bihéan village near which
I was staying heard I was going to Mashiko, though
they knew nothing of my object, they said, "Now
a messenger will be sent ahead to warn the slave-
traders that an Englishman is coming." The same
was told me by two Englishmen who traversed the
country last autumn for the mining concession, and
in my case I have not the slightest doubt that mes-
sengers were sent. Again, a Portuguese trader, living on the farther side of the Hungry Country, upon
the Mushi-Moshi (the Simoï, as the Portuguese clas-
sically call it), told me the drivers now bring the
slaves through unknown bush-paths north of the
old route. He kept a store which, being on the
edge of the Hungry Country, was as frequented and
lucrative as a wine-and-spirit house must be on the
frontier of a prohibition State. And he was the
only Portuguese I have met who recognized the
natives as fellow-subjects, and even as fellow-men,
with rights of their own. He also boasted, I think
justly, of the good effects of the war in 1902.

All these reasons may have contributed. But
still I think that the old caravan system has been
reduced within the last three years. The shock to
public feeling in Portugal owing to the Bailundu
war and its revelations; the disgrace of certain
officers at the forts, who were convicted of taking
a percentage of slaves from the passing caravans as

hush-money; the strong action of Captain Amorim in trying to suppress the whole traffic; the instructions to the forts to allow no chained gangs to pass —all these things have, I believe, acted as a check upon the old-fashioned methods. There is also an increased risk in obtaining slaves from the interior in large batches. The Belgians strongly oppose the entrance of the traders into their state, partly because guns and powder are the usual exchange for slaves, partly because they wish to retain their own natives under their own tender mercies. The line of Belgian forts along the frontier is quickly increasing. Some Bihéan traders have been shot. In one recent case, much talked of, a bullet from a Maxim gun struck the head of a gang of slaves, marching as usual in single file, and killed nine in succession. In any case, the traders seem to have discovered that the palmy days when they used to parade their chained gangs through the country, and burn, flog, torture, and cut throats as they pleased, are over for the present. For many months after the war even the traffic to San Thomé almost ceased. It has begun again now and is rapidly increasing. As I noted in a former letter, an order was issued in December, 1904, requiring the government agents to press on the supply. But at present, I think, the slaves are coming down in smaller gangs. They are not, as a rule, tortured; they are shackled only at night, and the traders take a certain amount of pains to conceal the whole traffic, or at least to make it look respectable.

As to secrecy, they are not entirely successful. A man whose word no one in Central Africa would think of doubting has just sent down notice from the interior that a gang of two hundred and fifty slaves passed through the Nanakandundu district, bound for the coast, in the end of February (1905), shackles and all. The man who brought the message had done his best to avoid the gang, fearing for his life. But there is no doubt they are coming through, and I ought to have met them near Mashiko if they had not taken a by-path or been broken up into small groups.

It was probably such a small group that I met within a day's journey of Caiala, the largest trading-house in Bihé. I was walking at about half an hour's distance from the road, when suddenly I came upon a party of eighteen or twenty boys and four men hidden in the bush. At sight of me they all ran away, the men driving the boys before them. But they left two long chicotes or sjamboks (hide whips) hanging on the trees, as well as the very few light loads they had with them. After a time I returned, and they ran away again. I then noticed that they posted a man on a tree-top to observe my movements, and he remained there till I trekked on with my own people. Of course the evidence is not conclusive, but it is suspicious. Men armed with chicotes do not hide a group of boys in the bush for nothing, and it is most probable that they formed part of a gang going into Bihé for sale.

I may have passed many such groups on my journey without knowing it, for it is a common trick of the traders now to get up the slaves as ordinary carriers. But among all of them, there was only one which was obviously a slave gang, almost without concealment. My carriers detected them at once, and I heard the word "apeka" (slaves)[1] passed down the line even before I came in sight of them. The caravan numbered seventy-eight in all. In front and rear were four men with guns, and there were six of them in the centre. The whole caravan was organized with a precision that one never finds among free carriers, and nearly the whole of it consisted of boys under fourteen. This in itself would be almost conclusive, for no trade caravan would contain anything like that proportion of boys, whereas boys are the most easily stolen from native villages in the interior, and, on the whole, they pay the cost of transport best. But more conclusive even than the appearance of the gang was the quiet evidence of my own carriers, who had no reason for lying, who never pointed out another caravan of slaves, and yet had not a moment's doubt as to this.

[1] Properly speaking, vapeka is the plural of upeka, a slave, but in Bihé apeka is used.

The importation of slaves from the interior into Angola may not be what it was. It may not be conducted under the old methods. There is no longer that almost continuous procession of chained and tortured men and women which all travellers who crossed the Hungry Country before 1902 describe. For the moment rubber has become almost as lucrative as man. The traffic has been driven underground. There is now a feeling of shame and risk about it, and the military authorities dare not openly give it countenance as before. But I have never heard of any case in which they openly interfered to stop it, and the thing still goes on. It is, in fact, fast recovering from the shock of the rebellion of 1902, and is now increasing again every month.

It will go on and it will increase as long as the authorities and traders habitually speak of the natives as "dogs," and allow the men under their command to misuse them at pleasure. To-day a negro soldier in the white Portuguese uniform seized a little boy at the head of my carriers, pounded his naked feet with the butt of his rifle, and was beating him unmercifully with the barrel, when I sprang upon him with two javelins which I happened to be carrying because my rifle was jammed. At sight of me the emblem of Portuguese justice crawled on the earth and swore he did not know it was a white man's caravan. That was sufficient excuse.

Three days ago word came to me on the march that one of my carriers had been shot at and wounded. We were in a district where three Chibokwe natives actually with shields and bows as well as guns had hung upon our line as we went in. I had that morning warned the carriers for the twentieth time that they must keep together, and had set an advanced and rear guard, knowing that stray carriers were being shot down. But natives are as incapable of organization as of seeing a straight line, and my people were straggled out helplessly over a length of five or six miles. Hurrying forward, I found that the bullet—a cube of copper—had just missed my carrier's head, had taken a chip out of his hand, and gone through my box. The carrier behind had caught the would-be murderer, and there he stood—a big Luvale man, with filed teeth, and head shaved but for a little tuft or pad at the top. I supposed he ought to be shot, but my rifle was jammed, and I am not a born executioner. However, I cleared a half-circle and set the man in the middle. A great terror came into his face as I went through the loading motions. I had determined, having blindfolded him, to catch him a full drive between the eyes. This would give him as great a shock as death. He would think it was death, and yet would have time to realize the horror of it afterwards, which in the case of death he would not have. But when all was ready, my carriers, including the wounded man, set up a great disturbance, and seized the muzzle of my rifle and turned it aside. They kept shouting some reason which I did not then understand. So I gave the punishment over to them, and they took the man's gun — a trade-gun or "Lazarino," studded with brass nails—stripped him of his powder-gourd, cloth, and all he had, beat him with the backs of their axes, and drove him naked into the forest, where he disappeared like a deer.

I found out afterwards that their reason for clemency was the fear of Portuguese vengeance upon their villages, because the man was employed by the fort at Mashiko, and therefore claimed the right of shooting any other native at sight, even over a minute's dispute about yielding the foot-path.

Such small incidents are merely typical of the attitude which the Portuguese take towards the natives and allow their own black soldiers and slaves to take. As long as this attitude is maintained, the immensely profitable slave-traffic which has filled with its horrors this route for centuries past will continue to fill it with horrors, no matter how secret or how legalized the traffic may become.

I have pitched my tent to-night on a hill-side not far from the fort of Matota, where a black sergeant and a few men are posted to police the middle of the Hungry Country. In front of me a deep stream is flowing down to the Zambesi with strong but silent current in the middle of a marsh. The air is full of the cricket's call and the other quiet sounds of night. Now and then a dove wakes to the brilliant moonlight, and coos, and sleeps again. Sometimes an owl cries, but no leopards are abroad, and it would be hard to imagine a scene of greater peace or of more profound solitude. And yet, along this path, there is no solitude, for the dead are here; neither is there any peace, but a cry.

VII

SAVAGES AND MISSIONS

THE Chibokwe do not sell their slaves; they kill them; and this distinction between them and the Bihéans is characteristic. The Bihéans are carriers and traders. They always have an eye fixed on the margin of profit. They will sell anything, including their own children, and it is waste to kill a man who may be sold to advantage. But the Chibokwe are savages of a wilder race, and no Bihéan would dare buy a Chibokwe slave, even if they had the chance. They know that the next Bihéan caravan would be cut to pieces on its way.

It is impossible to fix the limits of the Chibokwe country. The people are always on the move. It is partly the poverty of the land that drives them about, partly their habit of burning the village whenever the chief dies; and as villages go by the chief's name, they are the despair of geographers. But in entering the interior you may begin to be on your guard against the Chibokwe two days after crossing the Cuanza. They have a way of cutting off stray carriers, and, as I mentioned in my last

letter, my own little caravan was dogged by three
of them with shields and spears, who might have
been troublesome had they known that the Win-
chester with which I covered the rear was only useful as a club. It was in the Chibokwe country, too,
that the one attempt was made to rob my tent at
night, and again I only beat off the thieves by making a great display with a jammed rifle. On one
side their villages are mixed up with the Luimbi, on
the other with the Luena people and the Luvale,
who are scattered over the great, wet flats between
Mashiko and Nanakandundu. But they are a distinct people in themselves, and they appear to be
increasing and slowly spreading south. If the King
of Italy's arbitration gives the Zambesi tributaries
to England, the Chibokwe will form the chief part
of our new fellow-subjects, and will share the legal
advantages of Whitehall.[1]

They file or break their teeth into sharp points,
whereas the Bihéans compromise by only making
a blunt angle between the two in front. It used to
be said that pointed teeth were the mark of canni-
balism, but I think it more likely that these tribes
at one time had the crocodile or some sharp-toothed
fish as their totem, and certainly when they laugh
their resemblance to pikes, sharks, or crocodiles is

[1] Since this was written, the arbitration has been published
(July, 1905), but by the new frontier I think none of the Chibokwe will be brought under British influence.

very remarkable. Anyhow, the Chibokwe are not cannibals now, except for medicine, or in the hope of acquiring the moral qualities of the deceased. But I believe they eat the bodies of people killed by lightning or other sudden death, and the Bihéans do the same.

Though not so desert as the Hungry Country, the soil of their whole district is poor, and the people live in great simplicity. Hardly any maize is grown, and the chief food is the black bean, a meal pounded from yellow millet, and a beetle about four inches long. In all villages there are professional hunters and fishers, but game is scarce, and the fish in such rivers as the Mushi-Moshi (Simoï) are not allowed to grow much above the size of whitebait. Honey is to be found in plenty, but for salt, which is their chief desire, they have to put up with the ashes of a burned grass, unless they can buy real salt from the Bihéans in exchange for millet or rubber. Just at present rubber is their wealth, and they are doing rather a large trade in it. All over the forests they are grubbing up the plant by the roots, and in the villages you may hear the women pounding and tearing at it all the afternoon. But rubber thus extirpated gives a brief prosperity, and in two years, or five at the most, the rubber will be exhausted and the Chibokwe thrown back on their natural poverty.

In the arts they far surpass all their neighbors

on the west side. They are so artistic that the women wear little else but ornament. Their houses are square or oblong, with clean angles and straight sides, and the roofs, instead of being conical, are oblong too, having a straight beam along the top, like an English cottage. The tribe is specially famous for its javelins, spears, knives, hatchets, and other iron-work, which they forge in the open spaces round the village club-house, working up their little furnaces with wooden tubes and bellows of goat-skin, like loose drum-heads, pulled up and down with bits of stick to make a draught. A simple pattern is hammered on some of the axes, and on the side of one hut I saw an attempt at fresco—a white figure on a red ground under a white moon—the figure being quite sufficiently like an ox.

In dancing, the Chibokwe excel, like the Luvale people, who are their neighbors on the eastern side, farther in the interior, and their dances are much the same. It is curious that their favorite form is almost exactly like the well-known Albanian dance of the Greeks. Standing in a broken circle, they move round and round to a repeated song, while the leader sets the pace, and now and again springs out into the centre to display his steps. The Chibokwe introduce a few varieties, the man in the centre beckoning with his hand to any one in the ring to perform the next solo, and he in turn calling on another. There is also much more movement of the

body than in the Albanian dance, the chief object
of the art being to work the shoulders up and down,
and wriggle the backbone as much like a snake as
possible. But the general idea of the dance is the
same, and neither the movement nor the singing
nor the beat of the drum alters much throughout a
moonlit night.

It is natural that the Chibokwe should have re-
tained much of the religious feeling and rites which
the commercial spirit has destroyed in the Bihéans.
They are far more alive to the spiritual side of nature, and the fetich shrines are more frequent in all
their villages. The gate of every village, and, indeed, of almost every house, has its little cluster of
sticks, with antelope skulls stuck on the tops, or old
rags fluttering, or a tiny thatched roof covering a
patch of strewn meal. The people have a way of
painting the sticks in red and black stripes, and so
the fisher paints the rough model of a canoe that he
hangs by his door to please the fishing spirit. Or
sometimes he hangs a little net, and the hunter, besides his cluster of horned skulls, almost always
hangs up a miniature turtle three or four inches
long. I cannot say for what reason, but all these
charms are not to avert evil so much as to win the
favor of a benign spirit who loves to fish or hunt.
So far the rites are above the usual African religion
of terror or devil-worship. But when a woman with
child carves a wooden bird to hang over her door,

and gives it meal every evening and sprinkles meal in front of her door, I think her object is to ward off the spirits of evil from herself and her unborn baby.

In a Chibokwe village, one burning afternoon, I found a native woman being treated for sickness in the usual way. She was stretched on her back in the dust and dirt of the public place, where she had lain for four days. The sun beat upon her; the flies were thick upon her body. Over her bent the village doctor, assiduous in his care. He knew, of course, that the girl was suffering from witchcraft. Some enemy had put an evil spirit upon her, for in Africa natural death is unknown, and but for witchcraft and spirits man would be immortal. But still the doctor was trying the best human means he knew of as well. He had plastered the girl's body over with a compound of leaves, which he had first chewed into a pulp. He had then painted her forehead with red ochre, and was now spitting some white preparation of meal into her nose and mouth. The girl was in high fever—some sort of bilious fever. You could watch the beating of her heart. The half-closed eyes showed deep yellow, and the skin was yellow too. Evidently she was suffering the greatest misery, and would probably die next day.

It happened that two Americans were with me, for I had just reached the pioneer mission station at

Chinjamba, beyond Mashiko. One of them was a doctor, with ten years' experience in a great American city, and after commending the exertions of the native physician, he asked to be allowed to assist in the case himself. The native agreed at once, for the white man's fame as an exorcist had spread far through the country. Four or five days later I saw the same girl, no longer stretched on hot dust, no longer smeared with spittle, leaves, and paint, but smiling cheerfully at me as she pounded her meal among the other women.

The incident was typical of those two missionaries and their way of associating with the natives. It is typical of most young missionaries now. They no longer go about denouncing "idols" and threatening hell. They recognize that native worship is also a form of symbolism—a phase in the course of human ideas upon spiritual things. They do not condemn, but they say, "We think we know of better things than these," and the native is always willing to listen. In this case, for instance, after the girl had been put into a shady hut and doctored, the two missionaries sat down on six-inch native stools outside the club-house and began to sing. They were pioneers; they had only three hymns in the Chibokwe language, and they themselves understood hardly half the words. No matter; they took the meaning on trust. By continued repetition, by feeling no shame in singing a hymn twenty or thirty times over at one sitting, they had got the words fixed in the native minds, and when it came to the chorus the whole village shouted together like black stars. The missionaries understood the doctrine, the people understood the words; it was not a bad combination, and I thought those swinging choruses would never stop. The preaching was perhaps less exhilarating to the audience, but so it has sometimes been to other congregations, and the preacher's knowledge of the language he spoke was only five months old.

At the mission it was the same thing. The pioneers had set up a log hut in the forest, admitting the air freely through the floor and sides. They were living in hard poverty, but when they shared with me their beans and unleavened slabs of millet, it was pleasant to know that each of the two doors on either side of the hut was crammed with savage faces, eagerly watching the antics of civilization at meals. One felt like a lantern-slide, combining instruction with amusement. The audience consisted chiefly of patients who had built a camp of forty or fifty huts close outside the cabin, and came every morning to be cured—cured of broken limbs, bad insides, wounds, but especially of the terrible sores and ulcers which rot the shins and thighs, tormenting all this part of Africa. Among the patients were three kings, who had come far from the east. The greatest of them had brought a few wives—eight, I think—and some children, including a singularly fascinating princess with the largest smile I ever saw. Every morning the king came to my tent, showed me his goitre, asked for tobacco, and sat with me an hour in silent esteem. As I was not then accustomed to royalty, I was uncertain how three kings would behave themselves in hospital life; but in spite of their rank and station, they were quite good, and even smiled upon the religious services, feeling, no doubt, as all the rich feel, that such things were beneficial for the lower orders.

On certain evenings the missionaries went out into the hospital camp to sing and pray. They sat beside a log fire, which threw its light upon the black or copper figures crowding round in a thick half-circle—big, bony men, women shining with castor-oil, and swarms of children, hardly visible but for a sudden gleam of eyes and teeth. The three invariable hymns were duly sung—the chorus of the favorite being repeated seventeen times without a pause, as I once counted, and even then the people showed no sign of weariness. The woman next to me on that occasion sang with conspicuous enthusiasm. She was young and beautiful. Her mop of hair, its tufts solid with red mud, hung over her brow and round her neck, dripping odors, dripping oil. Her bare, brown arms jingled with copper bracelets, and at her throat she wore the section of round white shell which is counted the most precious ornament of all—"worth an ox," they say. Her little cloth was dark blue with a white pattern, and, squatted upon her heels, she held her baby between her thighs, stuffing a long, pointed breast into his mouth whenever he threatened to interrupt the music. For her whole soul was given to the singing, and with wide-open mouth she poured out to the stars and darkened forests the amazing words of the chorus:

> "Haleluyah! mwa aku kula,
> Jesu vene mwa aku sanga:"

There were two other lines, which I do not remember. The first line no one could interpret to me. The second means, "Jesus really loves me." The other two said, "His blood will wash my black heart white."

To people brought up from childhood in close familiarity with words like these there may be nothing astonishing about them. They have unhappily become the commonplaces of Christianity, and excite no more wonder than the sunrise. But I would give a library of theology to know what kind of meaning that brown Chibokwe woman found in them as she sat beside the camp-fire in the forest beyond the Hungry Country, and sang them seventeen times over to her baby and the stars.

When at last the singing stopped, one of the

missionaries began to read. He chose the first chapter of St. John, and in that savage tongue we listened to the familiar sentences, "In the beginning was the Word, and the Word was with God, and the Word was God." Again I looked round upon that firelit group of naked barbarians. I remembered the controversies of ages, the thinkers in Greek, the seraphic doctors, the Byzantine councillors, the saints and sinners of the intellect, Augustine in the growing Church, Faust in his study—all the great and subtle spirits who had broken their thought in vain upon that first chapter of St. John, and again I was filled with wonder. "For Heaven's sake, stop!" I felt inclined to cry. "What are these people to understand by 'the beginning'? What are we to understand by 'the Word'?" But when I looked again I recognized on all faces the mood of stolid acquiescence with which congregations at home allow the same words to pass over their heads year after year till they die as good Christians. So that I supposed it did not matter.

There seems to be a fascination to missionaries in St. John's Gospel, and, of course, that is no wonder. It is generally the first and sometimes the only part of the New Testament translated, and I have seen an old chief, who was diligently learning to read among a class of boys, spelling out with his black fingers such words as, "I am in the Father, and the Father in me." No doubt it may be said that religion has no necessary connection with the understanding, but I have sometimes thought it might be better to begin with something more comprehensible, both to savages and ourselves.

On points of this kind, of course, the missionaries may very well be right, but in one thing they are wrong. Most of them still keep up the old habit of teaching the early parts of the Old Testament as literal facts of history. But if there is anything certain in human knowledge, the Old Testament stories have no connection with the facts of history at all. No one believes they have. No scholar, no man of science, no theologian, no sane man would now think of accepting the Book of Genesis as a literal account of what actually happened when the world and mankind began to exist. Yet the missionaries continue to teach it all to the natives as a series of facts. I have heard one of the most experienced and influential of all the missionaries discussing with his highest class of native teachers whether all Persons of the Trinity were present at Eve's temptation; and when one of them asked what would have happened if Adam had refused to eat the apple, the class was driven to suppose that in that case men would have remained perfect, while women became as wicked as we see them now. It was a doctrine very acceptable to the native mind, but to hear those rather beautiful old stories still taught as the actual history of the world makes

137

one's brain whirl. One feels helpless and confused
and adrift from reason, as when another missionary,
whose name is justly famous, told me that there
were references to Moscow in Ezekiel, and Daniel
had exactly foretold the course of the Russo-Japa-
nese war. The native has enough to puzzle his
brain as it is. On one side he has the Christian ideal
of peace and good-will, of temperance and poverty
and honor and self-sacrifice, and of a God who is
love. And on the other side he has somehow to
understand the Christian's contumely, the Christian's incalculable injustice, his cruelty and deceit,
his insatiable greed for money, his traffic in human
beings whom the Christian calls God's children.
When the native's mind is hampered and entangled
in questions like these, no one has a right to increase his difficulties by telling him to believe primitive stories which, as historical facts, are no truer
than the native's own myths.

But, happily, matters of intellectual belief have
very little to do with personality, and many good
men have held unscientific views on Noah's Ark.
Contrary to nearly all travellers and traders in
Africa, I have nothing but good to say of the missionaries and their work. I have already mentioned
the order of the Holy Spirit and their great mission
at Caconda. The same order has two other stations
in South Angola and a smaller station among the
mountains of Bailundu, about two hours distant

from the fort and the American mission there. Its work is marked by the same dignity and quiet devotion as marks the work of all the orders wherever I have come across their outposts and places of danger through the world. It is constantly objected that the Portuguese have possessed this country for over four centuries, and have done nothing for the improvement or conversion of the natives, and I bear in mind those bishops of Loanda who sat on marble thrones upon the quay christening the slaves in batches as they were packed off by thousands to their misery in Cuba and Brazil. Both things are perfectly true. The Portuguese are not a missionary people. I have not met any but French, Alsatians, and Germans in the missions of the order out here. But that need not in the least diminish our admiration of the missions as they now are. Nor should we be too careful to remember the errors and cruelties of any people or Church in the past, especially when we reflect that England, which till quite lately was regarded as the great foe of slavery all over the world, was also the originator of the slave export, and that the supreme head of the Anglican Church was one of the greatest slave-traders ever known.

As to the scandals and sneers of traders, officials, and gold-prospectors against the missions, let us pass them by. They are only the weary old language of "the world." They are like the sneers of butchers and publicans at astronomy. They are the tribute of the enemy, the assurance that all is not in vain. It would be unreasonable to expect anything else, and dangerous to receive it. The only thing that makes me hesitate about the work of the order is that many traders and officials have said to me, "The Catholic missions are, at all events, practical; they do teach the natives carpentering and wagon-building and how to dig." It is perfectly true and admirable, and, as a matter of fact, the other missions do the same. But a mission might teach its followers to make wagons enough for a Boer's paradise and doors enough for all the huts in Africa and still have failed of its purpose.

Besides the order of the Holy Spirit, there are two other notable orders at work in Angola—the American mission (Congregationalist) under the "American Board," and the English mission (Plymouth Brethren) under divine direction only. Each mission has four stations, and each is about to start a new one. Some members of the English mission are Americans, like the pioneers at Chinjamba, and all are on terms of singular friendship, helping one another in every possible way, almost like the followers of Christ. Of all sects that I have ever known, these are the only two that I have heard pray for each other, and that without condemnation — I mean they pray in a different spirit from the Anglican prayer for Jews, Turks, infidels, and heretics.

There is another American order, called the Wesleyan Episcopalian, with stations at Loanda and among the grotesque mountains of Pungo Ndongo. English-speaking missionaries have now been at work in Loanda for nearly twenty-five years, and some of the pioneers, such as Mr. Arnot, Mr. Currie, Mr. Stover, Mr. Fay, and Mr. Sanders, are still directing the endeavor, with a fine stock of experience to guide them. They have outlived much abuse; they have almost outlived the common charge of political aims and the incitement of natives to rebellion, as in 1902. The government now generally leaves them alone. The Portuguese rob them, especially on the steamers and in the customs, but then the Portuguese rob everybody. Lately the American mission village at Kamundongo in Bihé has been set on fire at night three or four times, and about half of it burned down. But this appears to be the work of one particular Portuguese trader, who has a spite against the mission and sends his slaves from time to time to destroy it. An appeal to the neighboring fort at Belmonte would, of course, be useless. If the Chefe were to see justice done, the neighboring Portuguese traders would at once lodge a complaint at Benguela or Loanda, and he would be removed, as all Chefes are removed who are convicted of justice. But, as a rule, the missions are now left very much to themselves by the Portuguese, partly because the traders have found

out that some of the missionaries—four at least—
are by far the cleverest doctors in the country,
and nobody devotes his time to persecuting his
doctor.

As to the natives, it is much harder to judge their
attitude. Their name for a missionary is "afoola."
and though, I believe, the word only means a man
of learning, it naturally suggests an innocent simplicity—something "a bit soft," as we say. At
first that probably was the general idea, as was seen
when M. Coillard, the great French missionary of
Barotzeland, had a big wash in his yard one afternoon, and next Sunday preached to an enthusiastic
congregation all dressed in scraps of his own linen.
And to some extent the feeling still exists. There
are natives who go to a mission village for what
they can get, or simply for a sheltered existence and
kindly treatment. There are probably a good many
who experience religious convictions in order to
please, like the followers of any popular preacher
at home. But, as a rule, it is not comfort or gain,
it is not persuasive eloquence or religious conviction
that draws the native. It is the two charms of entire honesty and of inward peace. In a country
where the natives are habitually regarded as fair
game for every kind of swindle and deceit, where
bargains with them are not binding, and where
penalties are multiplied over and over again by
legal or illegal trickery, we cannot overestimate the

influence of men who do what they say, who pay
what they agree, and who never go back on their
word. From end to end of Africa common honesty
is so rare that it gives its possessor a distinction beyond intellect, and far beyond gold. In Africa any
honest man wins a conspicuous and isolated greatness. In twenty-five years the natives of Angola
have learned that the honesty of the missionaries is
above suspicion. It is a great achievement. It is
worth all the teaching of the alphabet, addition,
and Old Testament history, no matter how successful, and it is hardly necessary to search out any
other cause for the influence which the missionaries
possess.

So, as usual, it is the unconscious action that is
the best. Being naturally and unconsciously honest,
the missionaries have won the natives by honesty
—have won, that is to say, the almost imperceptible
percentage of natives who happen to live in the
three or four villages near their stations; and it
must be remembered that you might go through
Angola from end to end without guessing that missionaries exist. But, apart from this unconscious
influence, there are plenty of conscious efforts too.
There is the kindergarten, where children puddle in
clay and sing to movement and march to the tune
of "John Brown." There are schools for every
stage, and you may see the chief of a village doing
sums among the boys, and proudly declaring that for

his part $3 + 0 + 1$ shall equal five.[1] There are carpenters' shops and forges and brick-kilns and building classes and sewing classes for men. There are
Bible classes and prayer-meetings and church services where six hundred people will be jammed into
the room for four hundred, and men sweat, and
children reprove one another's behavior, and babies
yell and splutter and suck, and when service is over
the congregation rush with their hymn-books to
smack the mosquitoes on the walls and see the blood
spurt out. There are singing classes where hymns
are taught, and though the natives have nothing of
their own that can be called a tune, there is something horrible in the ease with which they pick up
the commonplace and inevitable English cadences.
I once had a set of carriers containing two or three
mission boys, and after the first day the whole lot
"went Fantee" on "Home, Sweet Home," just a
little wrong. For more than two years I have jour-
neyed over Africa in peace and war, but I have
never suffered anything to compare to that fortnight of "Home, Sweet Home," just a little wrong,
morning, noon, and night.

All these methods of instruction and guidance are
pursued in the permanent mission stations, to say

---

[1] It must be a little difficult to teach arithmetic to a race
whose word for "seven" is "six and two" (*epandu-vali*), or
"six over again." Or to teach dates where the word for "to-
morrow" (*hena*) is the same as the word for "yesterday."

nothing of the daily medical service of healing and surgery, which spreads the fame of the missions from village to village. Many out-stations, conducted by the natives themselves, have been formed, and they should be quickly increased, though it is naturally tempting to keep the sheep safe within the mission fold. If the missionaries were suddenly removed in a body, it is hard to say how long their teaching or influence would survive. My own opinion is that every trace of it would be gone in fifty or perhaps in twenty years. The Catholic forms would probably last longest, because greater use is made of a beautiful symbolism. But in half a century rum, slavery, and the oppression of the traders would have wiped all out, and the natives would sink into a far worse state than their original savagery. Whether the memory of the missions would last even fifty years would depend entirely upon the strength and number of the out-stations.

In practical life, the three great difficulties which the missions have to face are rum, polygamy, and slavery. From their own stations rum can be generally excluded, though sometimes a village is persecuted by a Portuguese trader because it will not buy his spirit. But the whole country is fast degenerating owing to rum. "You see no fine old men now," is a constant saying. Rum kills them off. It is making the whole people bloated and stupid. Near the coast it is worst, but the enormous amount carried into the interior or manufactured in Bihé is telling rapidly, and I see no hope of any change as long as rum plantations of cane or sweet-potato pay better than any others, and both traders and government regard the natives only as profitable swine.

As a matter of argument, polygamy is a more difficult question still. It is universally practised in Africa, and no native man or woman has ever had the smallest scruple of conscience or feeling of wrong about it. Where the natives can observe white men, they see that polygamy is in reality practised among them too. If they came to Europe or America, they would find it practised, not by every person, but by every nation under one guise or another. It seems an open question whether the native custom, with its freedom from concealment and its guarantees for woman's protection and support, is not better than the secret and hypocritical devices of civilization, under which only one of the women concerned has any protection or guarantee at all, while a man's relation to the others is nearly always stealthy, cruel, and casual. However, the missionaries, after long consideration, have decided to insist upon the rule of one man one wife for members of their Churches, and when I was at one station a famous Christian chief, Kanjumdu of Chiuka—by far the most advanced and intelligent native I have ever known—chose one wife out of his eight or ten, and married her with Christian rites, while the greater part of his twenty-four living children joined in the hymns. It was fine, but my sympathy was with one of the rejected wives, who would not come to the wedding-feast and refused to take a grain of meal or a foot of cloth from his hand ever again.

As to slavery, I have already spoken about the missionaries' attitude. They dare not say anything openly against it, because if they published the truth they would probably be poisoned and certainly be driven out of the country, leaving their followers exposed to a terrible and exterminating persecution. So they help in what few special cases they can, and leave the rest to time and others. It is difficult to criticise men of such experience, devotion, and singleness of aim. One must take their judgment. But at the same time one cannot help remembering that a raging fire is often easier to deal with than a smouldering refuse-heap, and that in spite of all the blood and sorrow, the wildest revolution on behalf of justice has never really failed.

But, as I said, it is hard for me to criticise the missionaries out here. My opinion of them may be misguided by the extraordinary kindliness which only traders and officials can safely resist, and I suppose one ought to envy the reasonableness of such people when, after enjoying the full hospitality

147

of the mission stations, they spend the rest of their time in sneering at the missionaries. Nothing can surpass mission hospitality. The stranger's condition, poverty, or raggedness does not matter in the least, nor does the mission's own scarcity or want. Whatever there is belongs to the strangers, even if nothing is left but a dish of black beans and a few tea-leaves, used already. In a long and wandering life I have nowhere found hospitality so complete and ungrudging and unconscious. Only those who have lived for months among the dirt and cursing of ox-wagons, or have tramped with savages far through deserts wet and dry, plunged in slime or burned with thirst, worn with fever and poisoned with starvation, could appreciate what it means to come at last into a mission station and see the trim thatched cottages, like an old English village, and to hear the quiet and pleasant voices, and feel again the sense of inward peace, which, I suppose, is the reward of holy living. How often when I have been getting into bed the night after I have thus arrived, I have thought to myself, "Here I am, free from hunger and thirst, in a silent room, with a bed and real sheets, while people at home probably picture me dying in the depths of a dismal forest where pygmies sharpen their poisoned arrows and make their saucepans ready, or a lion stands rampant on one side of me, and, on the other side, a unicorn."

VIII

THE SLAVE ROUTE TO THE COAST

AFTER coming out from the interior by passing again through the Hungry Country from the Zambesi basin to the Cuanza I determined to continue following the old slave route down to Benguela and the sea. I have already spoken of this route as the main road of Central Africa, and the two hundred and seventy or three hundred miles of it which connect Bihé with the coast are crowded with trade, especially at the beginning of the dry season, which was the time of my journey. It is only a carrier's track, though the Portuguese, as their habit is, have forced the natives to construct a few miles of useless road here and there, at intervals of several days' march. But along that winding track, sometimes so steep and difficult that it is like a goat-path in the Alps, thousands of carriers pass every year, bearing down loads of rubber and beeswax, and bringing back cotton, salt, tinned foods, and, above all, rum. It is against the decree of the Brussels Conference of 1890 to introduce rum into Bihé at all, but who cares about decrees when rum pays and no one takes the trouble to shoot? And down this winding track the export slaves have been driven century after century. I suppose the ancestors of half the negroes in the United States and of nearly all in Cuba and Brazil came down it. And thousands of export slaves still come down it every year. Laws and conferences have prohibited the slave-trade for generations past, but who cares about laws and conferences as long as slavery pays and no one takes the trouble to shoot?

How the traffic is worked may be seen from some things which I observed upon my way. Being obliged to wait at various places to arrange carriers and recover from fevers, I spent about five weeks on the road from the crossing of the Cuanza to the sea, though it can be done in three weeks, or even in seventeen days. For the first few days I was back again in the northern part of the Bihé district, and I early passed the house of a Portuguese trader of whose reputation I had heard before. He is still claiming enormous damages for injury to his property in the war of 1902. The villagers have appealed to the fort at Belmonte against the amount, but are ordered to pay whatever he asks. To supply the necessary rubber and oxen they have now pawned their children into slavery without hope of redemption. Two days before I passed the house a villager, having pawned the last of his children and possessing nothing else, had shot himself in the bush close by. Things like that make no difference to the trader. It is the money he wants. The damage done to his property three years ago must be paid for twentyfold. Still, he is not simply the "economic man" of the old text-books. He has a decadent love of art, distinct from love of money, and just before I passed his house he had summoned the chiefs of the village as though for a conference, had locked them up in his compound, and every night he was making the old men dance for his pleasure. To the native mind such a thing is as shocking as it would be to Englishmen if Mr. Beit or Mr. Eckstein kept the Lord Chancellor and the Archbishop of Canterbury to gambol naked before him on Sunday afternoons.

So the matter stands, and the villagers must go on selling more and more of their wives and children that the white man's greed may be satisfied.

A day or two farther on I turned aside from the main track to visit one of the agents whom the government has specially appointed to conduct the purchase of slaves for the islands of San Thomé and Principe. There are two agents officially recognized in the Bihé district. On my way I met an old native notorious for a prosperous career of slave-trading. At the moment he was leading along a finely built man by a halter round his neck, but at sight of me he dropped the end of rope. A man who was with me charged him at once with having just sold two of his own slaves—a man and a woman—for San Thomé. He protested with righteous indignation. He would never think of doing such a thing! Sell for San Thomé! He would even give a long piece of cloth to rescue a native from such a fate! Yet, beyond question, he had sold the man and woman to the Agent that morning. They were at the Agent's house when I arrived, and I was told he had only failed to sell the other slave because his price was too high.

The Agent himself was polite and hospitable. Business was pretty brisk. I knew he had sent off eight slaves to the coast only three days before, with orders that they should carry their own shackles and be carefully pinned together at night. But we talked only of the rumored division of the Congo, for on the other subject he was naturally a little shy, and I found out long afterwards that he knew the main object of my journey.[1] Next day,

---

[1] I am not quite sure how this was discovered—whether an indiscreet friend "gave me away," or whether an indiscreet letter was opened in the post, or the traders were simply guided by conjecture and a guilty conscience. At all events, one of the principal slave-dealers in Bihé discovered it, and took the pains to publish reports against me, that reached as far as Mossamedes. The English and American missions were actually warned to have nothing to do with me because I was a Jesuit in disguise, and had come to destroy their work! Further on I may have to refer to the plots to assassinate me on the coast during the voyage home, but I mention these little personal matters only to show that the slave-traders had been put

however, he was alone with the friend who had accompanied me, and he then attempted to defend his position as Agent by saying the object of the government was to buy up slaves through their special agents and "redeem" them from slavery by converting them into "contract laborers" for San Thomé. The argument was ingenious. The picture of a pitiful government willing to purchase the freedom of all slaves without thought of profit, and only driven to contract them for San Thomé because otherwise the expense would be unbearable—it is almost pathetic. But the Agent knew, as every one out here knows, that the people whom the government buys and "redeems" have been torn from their homes and families on purpose to be "redeemed"; that but for the purchases by the government agents for San Thomé the whole slave-traffic would fall to pieces; and that the actual condition of these "contracted laborers" upon the islands does not differ from slavery in any point of importance.

Leaving on the right the volcanic district of North Bihé, with its boiling springs and great deposits of magnesia, the path to the coast continues to run westward and a point or two south through country typical of Africa's central plateau. There are the usual wind-swept spaces of bog and yellow grass,

on their guard and would naturally try to conceal as much as they could of their traffic's horror, and that is the chief reason why I met no gangs of slaves in chains.

the usual rolling lines of scrubby forest, and the shallow valleys with narrow channels of water running through morass. The path skirts the northern edge of the high, wet plain of Bouru-Bouru, and on the same day, after passing this, I saw far away in the west a little blue point of mountain, hanging like an island upon the horizon. A few hours afterwards bare rock began to appear through the bog-earth and sand of the forest, and next morning new mountains came into sight from hour to hour as I advanced, till there was quite a cluster of little blue islands above the dark edges of the trees.

The day after, when I had been walking for about two hours through the monotonous woods, the upland suddenly broke. It was quick and unexpected as the snapping of a bowstring, and far below me was revealed a great expanse of country—broad valleys leading far away to the west and north, isolated groups of many-colored mountains, bare and shapely hills of granite and sandstone, and one big, jagged tooth or pike of purple rock, rising sheer from a white plain thinly sprinkled with trees and marked with watercourses. The whole scene, bare and glowing under the cloudless sky of an African winter, was like those delicate landscapes in nature's most friendly wilderness which the Umbrians used to paint as backgrounds to the Baptist or St. Jerome or a Mother and Child. To one who has spent many months among the black forest, the marshes and

sand-hills of Bihé and the Hungry Country, it gleams
with a radiance of jewels, and is full of the inward
stir and longing that the sudden vision of mountains
always brings.[1]

At the top of the hill was a large sweet-potato
plantation for rum. A gang of twenty-three slaves
—chiefly women—was clearing a new patch from
the bush for an extension of the fields. Over them,
as usual, stood a Portuguese ganger, who encouraged their efforts with blows from a long black
chicote, or hippo whip, which he rapidly tried to
conceal down his trousers leg at sight of me.

At the foot of the hill, where a copious stream of
water ran, a similar rum-factory had just been constructed. The hideous main building—gaunt as a
Yorkshire mill—the whitewashed rows of slave-
huts, the newly broken fields, the barrels just beginning to send out a loathsome stench of new
spirit—all were as fresh and vile as civilization could
make them. As we passed, the slaves were just enjoying a holiday for the burial of one of their number who had died that morning. They were gathered in a large crowd round the grave on the edge
of the bush. Presently six of them brought out the
body, wrapped in an old blanket, rolled it sideways
into the shallow trench, and covered it up with
earth and stones. As we climbed the next hill,

[1] See Commander Cameron's description of the same view in
1876: *Across Africa*, p. 459.

my carriers, who were much interested, kept saying to one another: "Slaves! Poor slaves!" Then we heard a bell ring. The people began to crawl back to their work. The slaves' holiday was over.

We had now passed from Bihé into the district of Bailundu, and the mountains stood around us as we descended, their summits rising little higher than the level of the Bihéan plateau — say five to six thousand feet above the sea. A detached hill in front of us was conspicuous for its fortified look. From the distance it was like one of the castellated rocks of southern France. It was the old Umbala, or king's fortress, of Bailundu, and here the native kings used to live in savage magnificence before the curse of the white men fell. On the summit you still may see the king's throne of three great rocks, the heading-stone where his enemies suffered, the stone of refuge to which a runaway might cling and gain mercy by declaring himself the king's slave, the royal tombs with patterned walls hidden in a depth of trees, and the great flat rock where the women used to dance in welcome to their warriors returning from victory. One day I scrambled up and saw it all in company with a man who remembered the place in its high estate and had often sat beside the king in judgment. But all the glory is departed now. The palace was destroyed and burned in 1896. The rock of refuge and the royal throne are grown over with tall grasses. Leopards and snakes possess them merely, and it is difficult even to fight one's way up the royal ascent through the tangle of the creepers and bush.[1]

At the foot of the hill, within a square of ditch and rampart, stands the Portuguese fort, the scene of the so-called "Bailundu war" of 1902. It was here that the native rising began, owing to a characteristic piece of Portuguese treachery, the Commandant having seized a party of native chiefs who were visiting him, at his own invitation, under promise of peace and safe-conduct. The whole affair was paltry and wretched. The natives displayed their usual inability to combine; the Portuguese displayed their usual cowardice. But, as I have shown before, the effect of the outbreak was undoubtedly to reduce the horrors of the slave-trade for a time. The overwhelming terror of the slave-traders and other Portuguese, who crept into hiding to shelter their precious lives, showed them they had gone too far. The atrocious history of Portuguese cruelty and official greed which reached Lisbon at last did certainly have some effect upon the national conscience. As I have mentioned in earlier letters, Captain Amorim of the artillery was sent out to mitigate the abominations of the trade, and for a time, at all events, he succeeded. Owing to terror, the export of slaves to San Thomé ceased altogether

[1] Cameron visited King Congo there in 1876: *Across Africa*, p. 460.

for about six months after the rising. It has gone
back to its old proportions now—the numbers aver-
aging about four thousand head a year (not including babies), and gradually rising.[1] But since then
the traders have not dared to practise the same
open cruelties as before, and the new regulations for
slave-traffic—known as the Decree of January 29,
1903—do, at all events, aim at tempering the worst
abuses, though their most important provisions are
invariably evaded.

Only a mile or two from the fort, and quite visible
from the rocks of the old Umbala, stands the American mission village of Bailundu—I believe the oldest mission in Angola except the early Jesuits'. It
was founded in 1881, and for more than twenty
years has been carried on by Mr. Stover and Mr.
Fay, who are still conducting it. The Portuguese
instigated the natives to drive them out once, and
have wildly accused them of stirring up war, protecting the natives, and other crimes. But the
mission has prospered in spite of all, and its village
is now, I think, the prettiest in Angola. How long
it may remain in its present beautiful situation one
cannot say. Twenty years ago it was surrounded

---

[1] The official numbers of slaves exported to San Thomé for
the first four months of 1905 are: January, 369; February, 349;
March, 366; April, 302—a rate which would give a total of 4158
for the year. In June I travelled by a ship which took 273
slaves to San Thomé and Principe, and there are two slave-
ships a month.

only by natives, but now the Portuguese have crept
up to it with their rum and plantations and slavery,
and where the Portuguese come neither natives nor
missions can hope to stay long. It may be that in
a year or two the village will be deserted, as the
American mission village of Saccanjimba, a few days
farther east, has lately been deserted, and the houses
will be occupied by Portuguese convicts with a
license to trade, while the church becomes a rum-
store. In that case the missionaries will be wise to
choose a place outside the fifty-kilometre radius
from a fort, beyond which limit no Portuguese trader
may settle. So true it is that in modern Africa an
honest man has only the whites to fear. But unhappily new forts are now being constructed at two
or three points along this very road.

Soon after leaving Bailundu the track divides,
and one branch of it runs northwest, past the foot
of that toothed mountain, or pike,[1] and so at length
reaches the coast at Novo Redondo—a small place
with a few sugar-cane plantations for rum and a
government agency for slaves. I am told that on
this road the slaves are worse treated and more
frequently shackled than upon the path I followed,
and certainly Novo Redondo is more secret and
freer from the interference of foreigners than Benguela. But I think there cannot really be much

[1] Cameron called it "The Devil's Finger": *Across Africa*,
p. 464.

difference. The majority of slaves are still brought down the old Benguela route, and scattered along it at intervals I have found quite new shackles, still used for pinning the slaves together, chiefly at night, though it is true the shackles near the coast are not nearly so numerous as in the interior.

I was myself determined to follow the old track and come down to the sea by that white path where I had seen the carriers ascending and descending the mountains above Katumbella many months before. Within two days from Bailundu I entered a notorious lion country. Lions are increasing rapidly all along the belt of mountains here, and they do not hesitate to eat mankind, making no prejudiced distinction between white and black. Their general method is to spring into a rest-hut at night and drag off a carrier, or sometimes two, while the camp is asleep. All the rest-camps in this district are strongly stockaded with logs, twelve or fourteen feet high, but carriers are frequently killed in spite of all the stockade. There is one old lion who has made quite a reputation as a man-hunter, and if he had an ancestral hall he could decorate it with the "trophies" of about fifty human heads. He has chosen for his hunting-lodge some cave near the next fort westward from Bailundu, and there at eve he may sometimes be seen at play upon the green. Two officers are stationed in the fort, but they do not care to interfere with the creature's habits and pursuits. They do not even train their little toy gun on him. Perhaps they are humanitarians. So he devours mankind at leisure.

When we camped near that fort, my boys insisted I should sleep in a hut inside the stockade instead of half a mile away from them as usual. The huts are made of dry branches covered with dry leaves and grass. Inside that stockade I counted over forty huts, and each hut was crammed with carriers—men, women, and children—for the dry-season trade was beginning. There must have been five or six hundred natives in that camp at night. The stockade rose fourteen feet or more and was impenetrable. The one gate was sealed and barred with enormous logs to keep out the lion. I was myself given a hut in the very centre of the camp as an honor. And in every single hut around me a brilliant fire was lighted for cooking and to keep the carriers warm all night. One spark gone wrong would have burned up the whole five hundred of us without a chance of escape. So when we came to the stockaded camp of the next night I pitched my tent far outside it as usual, and listened to the deep sighing and purring of the lions with great indifference, while the boys marvelled at a rashness which was nothing to their own.

As one goes westward farther into the mountains, the path drops two or three times by sudden, steep descents, like flights of steps down terraces, and at

each descent the air becomes closer and the plants
and beasts more tropical, till one reaches the deep
valleys of the palm, the metallic butterfly, and thousands of yellow monkeys. Beside the route great
masses of granite rise, weathered into smooth and
unclimbable surface, like the Matopo hills. The
carriers from the high interior suffer a good deal
at each descent. "We have lost our proper breathing," they say, and they pine till they return to the
clearer air. It is here that many of the slaves try
to escape. If they got away, there would not be
much chance for them among the shy and apelike
natives of the mountain belt, who remain entirely
savage and are reputed to be cannibal still. But
the slaves try to escape, and are generally brought
back to a fate worse than being killed and eaten.
On May 17th, five days above Katumbella, I met one
of them who had been caught. He was a big Luvale man, naked, his skin torn and bleeding from
his wild rush through thorns and rocks. In front
and behind him marched one of his owner's slaves
with drawn knives or matchets, two feet long, ready
to cut him down if he tried to run again. I asked
my boys what would happen to him, and they said
he would be flogged to death before the others. I
cannot say. I should have thought he was too
valuable to kill. He must have been worth over
£20 as he stood, and £30 when landed at San Thomé.
But, of course, the trader may have thought it would

pay better to flog him to death as an example. True, it is not always safe to kill a slave. Last April a man in Benguela flogged a slave to death with a hippo whip, and, no doubt to his great astonishment, he found himself arrested and banished for a time to Mozambique—"the other coast," as it is called—a far from salubrious home. But five days' inland along the caravan route the murderer of a slave would be absolutely secure, if he did not mind the loss of the money.

Two days later I met another of those vast caravans of natives, one of which I had seen just the other side of the Cuanza. This caravan numbered nearly seven hundred people, and, under the protection of an enormous Portuguese banner, they were marching up into the interior with bales and stores, wives and children, intending to be absent at least two years for trade. These large bodies of men are a great source of supply to the government slave-agents; for when they find two tribes at war, they hire themselves out to fight for one on condition of selling the captives from the other, and so they secure an immense profit for themselves, while pleasing their allies and bringing an abundance of slaves for the Portuguese government to "redeem" by sending them to labor at San Thomé till their lives end.

The next day's march brought us to a straight piece of valley, where such a number of rest-huts have been gradually built that the place looks like a large native village. All the little paths from the interior meet here, because it stands at the mouth of a long and very deep valley, sometimes called the cañon, by which alone the next belt of dry and mountainous country can be crossed. The water is dirty and full of sulphur, but it has to be carried in gourds for the next day's march, because for twenty-five miles there is no water at all.

Natives here come down from the nearest villages and sell sweet-potatoes and maize to the carriers in exchange for salt and chips of tobacco or sips of rum, so that at this season, when the carriers every night number a thousand or more, there is something like a fair. Mixed up with the carriers are the small gangs of slaves, who are collected here in larger parties before being sent on to the coast.

With the help of one of my boys I had some conversation that evening with a woman who was kept waiting for other gangs, just as I was kept waiting because fever made me too weak to move. She was a beautiful woman of about twenty or little more, with a deep-brown skin and a face of much intelligence, full of sorrow. She had come from a very long way off, she said—far beyond the Hungry Country. She thought four moons had gone since they started. She had a husband and three children at home, but was seized by the men of another tribe and sold to a white man for twenty cartridges. She did not know what kind of cartridges they were—they were "things for a gun." Her last baby was very young, very young. She was still suckling him when they took her away. She did not know where she was going. She supposed it was to Okalunga—a name which the natives use equally for hell or the abyss of death, the abyss of the sea and for San Thomé. She was perfectly right. She was one of the slaves who had been purchased, probably on the Congo frontier, on purpose for the Portuguese government's agent to "redeem" and send to the plantations. It is a lucrative business to supply such philanthropists with slaves. And it is equally lucrative for the philanthropists to redeem them.

The long, dry cañon, where the carriers have to climb like goats from rock to rock along the steep mountain-side, with fifty or sixty pounds on their heads, brought us at last to a brimming reach of the Katumbella River. It is dangerous both from hippos and crocodiles; though the largest crocodiles I have ever seen were lower down the river, on the sand-banks close to its mouth, where they devour women and cattle, and lie basking all their length of twenty to thirty feet, just like the dragons of old. From the river the path mounts again for the final day's march through an utterly desert and waterless region of mountain ridges and stones and sand, sprinkled with cactus and aloes and a few gray thorns. But, like all this mountain region, the desert gives ample shelter to eland, koodoo, and other deer. Buffaloes live there, too, and in very dry seasons they come down at night to drink at the river pools close to the sea.

The sea itself is hidden from the path by successive ridges of mountain till the very last edge is reached. On the morning of my last day's trek a heavy, wet mist lay over all the valleys, and it was only when we climbed that we could see the mountain-tops, rising clear above it in the sunshine. But before mid-day the mist had gone, and, looking back from a high pass, I had my last view over the road we had travelled, and far away towards the interior of the strange continent I was leaving. Then we went on westward, and climbed the steep and rocky track over the final range, till at last a great space of varied prospect lay stretched out below us—the little houses of Katumbella at our feet, the fertile plain beside its river green with trees and plantations; on our right the white ring of Lobito Bay, Angola's future port; on our left a line of yellow beach like a road leading to the little white church and the houses of Benguela, fifteen miles away; and beyond them again to the desert promontory, with grotesque rocks. And there, far away in front, like a vast gulf of dim and misty blue, merging in the sky without a trace of horizon, stretched the sea itself; and to an Englishman the sea is always the way home.

So, as I had hoped, I came down at last from the mountains into Katumbella by that white path which has been consecrated by so much misery. And as I walked through the dimly lighted streets and beside the great court-yards of the town that night, I heard again the blows of the palmatoria and chicote and the cries of men and women who were being "tamed."

"I do not trouble to beat my slaves much—I mean my contracted laborers," said the trader who was with me. "If they try to run away or anything, I just give them one good flogging, and then sell them to the Agent for San Thomé. One can always get £16 per head from him."

A few days afterwards, on the Benguela road, I passed a procession of forty-three men and women, marching in file like carriers, but with no loads on their heads. Four natives in white coats and armed with guns accompanied them, ready to shoot down any runaway. The forty-three were a certain company's detachment of "voluntary laborers" on their way to the head "Emigration Agent" at Benguela and to the ship for San Thomé. Third among them marched that woman who had been taken from her husband and three children and sold for twenty cartridges.

Thus it is that the islands of San Thomé and Principe have been rendered about the most profitable bits of the earth's surface, and England and America can get their chocolate and cocoa cheap.

IX

THE EXPORTATION OF SLAVES

WHEN I was up in the interior, I had always intended to wait a while on the coast, if ever I should reach it again, in order to watch the process of the conversion of slaves into "contracted laborers" according to law. So it was fortunate that, owing to the delays of fevers and carriers, I succeeded in just missing a steamer bound for San Thomé and home. Fortunate, because the temptation to go straight on board would have been very strong, since I was worn with sickness, and within two days of reaching Katumbella I learned that special dangers surrounded me, owing to the discovery of my purpose by the Portuguese traders. As a matter of fact, I might have caught the ship by pushing my carriers on without a pause, but the promptings of conscience, supported by a prospect of the best crocodile-shooting that man can enjoy, induced me to run the risk of assassination and stay.

So I stayed on the coast for nearly three weeks, seeing what I could, hunting crocodiles, and devising schemes for getting my papers home even if

I should never reach home myself. One of the first
things I saw was a procession of slaves who had just
been "redeemed" into "contracted laborers," and
were being marched off in the early morning sunlight from Katumbella to Lobito Bay, there to be
embarked for San Thomé on the ship which I had
missed.[1] It so happened that this ship put in at
Lobito Bay, which lies only some eight miles north
from Katumbella down a waterless spit of sand, as
I have before described, and there can be no doubt
that this practice will become more and more common as the railway from the new port progresses.
Katumbella, united with the bay, will become the
main depot for the exportation of slaves and other
merchandise, while Benguela, having no natural
harbor, will gradually fall to ruin. At present, I
suppose, the government Agent for slaves at Benguela, together with the Curador, whose act con-
verts them into contract laborers, comes over for
the occasion whenever the slaves are to be shipped

[1] I find that the latest published Consular Report on San
Thomé and Principe (1902) actually repeats the hypocritical
fiction about the redemption of slaves. After speaking of the
"enormous mortality" on the two islands, the Report continues: "So large a death-rate calls for constant fresh supplies
of laborers from Angola, the principal ports from which they
are obtained being Benguela, Novo Redondo, and Loanda,
where they are ransomed from the black traders who bring them
from the far interior." Mr. Consul Nightingale, who wrote the
Report, was, of course, perfectly aware of the truth, and no
doubt he wrote in irony. But English people do not understand irony—least of all in an official document.

from Lobito Bay, just as in England a bishop travels from place to place for Confirmations as required.

Bemused with a parting dole of rum, bedecked in brilliantly striped jerseys, grotesque caps, and flashy loin-cloths to give them a moment's pleasure, the unhappy throng were escorted to their doom, the tin tickets with their numbers and the tin cylinders with their form of contract glittering round their necks or at their sides. Men and women were about equal in number, and some of the women carried babes lashed to their backs; but there were no older children. The causes which had brought these men and women to their fate were probably as different as the lands from which they came. Some had broken native customs or Portuguese laws, some had been charged with witchcraft by the medicine-man because a relative died, some could not pay a fine, some were wiping out an ancestral debt, some had been sold by uncles in poverty, some were the indemnity for village wars; some had been raided on the frontier, others had been exchanged for a gun; some had been trapped by Portuguese, others by Bihéan thieves; some were but changing masters, because they were "only good for San Thomé," just as we in London send an old cab-horse to Antwerp. I cannot give their history. I only know that about two hundred of them, muddled with rum and bedecked like clowns, passed along that May morning to a land of doom from which there was no return.

It was June 1st when, as I described in my last letter, I met that other procession of slaves on their way from Katumbella to Benguela, in readiness for embarkation in the next ship, which did not happen to stop at Lobito Bay. It was a smaller gang— only forty-three men and women—for it was the result of only one Agent's activity, though, to be sure, he was the leading and most successful Agent in Angola. They marched under escort, but without loads and without chains, though the old custom of chaining them together along that piece of road is still commonly practised—I suppose because the fifteen miles of country through which the road leads, when once the small slave-plantations round Katumbella have been passed, is a thorny desert where a runaway might easily hide, hoping to escape by sea or find cover in the towns. I have myself seen the black soldiers or police searching the bush there for fugitives, and once I found a Portuguese dying of fever among the thorns, to which he had fled from what is roughly called justice.[1]

By the time I saw that second procession I was myself living in Benguela, and was able to follow

[1] There is a well-known carriers' song with the refrain, "She has crossed Ondumba ya Maria," that being the name of a dry brook on this road from Katumbella to Benguela. It means, "She has gone into slavery to be sold for San Thomé"—"Gone to the devil," or, "Gone to glory," as we say, almost indifferently.

the slave's progress almost point by point, in spite of the uncomfortable suspicion with which I was naturally regarded. Writing of the town before, I mentioned the large court-yards with which nearly every house is surrounded—memorials of the old days when this was the central depot for the slave-trade with Brazil. In most cases these court-yards are now used as resting-places for the free carriers who have brought products from the interior and are waiting till the loads of cloth and rum are ready for the return journey. But the trading-houses that go in for business in "serviçaes" still put the court-yards to their old purpose, and confine the slaves there till it is time to get them on board.

A day or two before the steamer is due to depart a kind of ripple seems to pass over the stagnant town. Officials stir, clerks begin to crawl about with pens, the long, low building called the Tribunal opens a door or two, a window or two, and looks quite busy. Then, early one morning, the Curador arrives and takes his seat in the long, low room as representing the beneficent government of Portugal. Into his presence the slaves are herded in gangs by the official Agent. They are ranged up, and in accordance with the Decree of January 29, 1903, they are asked whether they go willingly as laborers to San Thomé. No attention of any kind is paid to their answer. In most cases no answer is given. Not the slightest notice would be taken of a refusal.

The legal contract for five years' labor on the island of San Thomé or Principe is then drawn out, and, also in accordance with the Decree, each slave receives a tin disk with his number, the initials of the Agent who secured him, and in some cases, though not usually at Benguela, the name of the island to which he is destined. He also receives in a tin cylinder a copy of his register, containing the year of contract, his number and name, his birthplace, his chief's name, the Agent's name, and "observations," of which last I have never seen any. Exactly the same ritual is observed for the women as for the men. The disks are hung round their necks, the cylinders are slung at their sides, and the natives, believing them to be some kind of fetich or "white man's Ju-ju," are rather pleased. All are then ranged up and marched out again, either to the compounds, where they are shut in, or straight to the pier where the lighters, which are to take them to the ship, lie tossing upon the waves.

The climax of the farce has now been reached. The deed of pitiless hypocrisy has been consummated. The requirements of legalized slavery have been satisfied. The government has "redeemed" the slaves which its own Agents have so diligently and so profitably collected. They went into the Tribunal as slaves, they have come out as "contracted laborers." No one in heaven or on earth can see the smallest difference, but by the change of name Portugal stifles the enfeebled protests of nations like the English, and by the excuse of law she smooths her conscience and whitens over one of the blackest crimes which even Africa can show.

Before I follow the slaves on board, I must raise one uncertain point about the Agents. I am not quite sure on what principle they are paid. According to the Decree of 1903, they are appointed by the local committee in San Thomé, consisting of four officials and three planters, chosen by the central government Committee of Emigration in Lisbon. The local committee has to fix the payment due to each Agent, and of course the payment is ultimately made by the planters, who requisition the local committee for as many slaves as they require, and pay in proportion to the number they receive. Now a planter in San Thomé gives from £26 to £30 for a slave delivered on his plantation in good condition. The Agent at Benguela will give £16 for any healthy man or woman brought to him, but he rarely goes up to £20. From this considerable profit balance of £10 to £14 per head there are, it is true, certain deductions to be made. By the Decree, each Agent has to pay the government £100 deposit before he sets up in the slave-dealing business, and most probably he recoups himself out of the profits. For his license he has to pay the government two shillings a slave (with a minimum payment of £10 a year). Also to the government he pays £1 per slave in stamp duty, and six shillings on the completion of each contract. He has further to pay a tax of six shillings per slave to the port of landing, and from the balance of profit we must also deduct the slave's fare on the steamer from Benguela to San Thomé. This, I believe, is £2— a sum which goes to enrich the happy shareholders in the "Empreza Nacional," who last year (1904) received twenty-two per cent. on their money as profit from the slave-ships. Then the captain of the steamer gets four shillings and the doctor two shillings for every slave landed alive, and, on an average, only four slaves per hundred die on the voyage, which takes about eight days. There are probably other deductions to be made. The Curador will get something for his important functions. There are stories that the commandants of certain forts still demand blackmail from the processions of slaves as they go by. I was definitely told that the commandant of a fort very near to Benguela always receives ten shillings a head, but I cannot say if that is true.

In any case, at the very lowest, there is £4 to be deducted for fare, taxes, etc., from the apparent balance of £10 to £14 per slave. But even then the profit on each man or woman sold is considerable, and the point that I am uncertain about is whether the Agent at Benguela and his deputies in Novo Redondo and Bihé pocket all the profit they can possibly make, or are paid a fixed proportion of the average profits by the local committee at San Thomé. The latter would be in accordance with the Decree; the other way more in accordance with Portuguese methods.

Unhappily I was not able to witness the embarkation of the slaves myself, as I had been poisoned the night before and was suffering all day from violent pain and frequent collapse, accompanied by extreme cold in the limbs.[1] So that when, late in the evening, I crawled on board at last, I found the slaves already in their place on the ship. We were taking only one hundred and fifty of them from Benguela, but we gathered up other batches as we went along, so that finally we reached a lucrative cargo of two hundred and seventy-two (not counting babies), and as only two of them died in the week, we landed two hundred and seventy safely on the islands. This was perhaps rather a larger number than usual, for the steamers, which play the part of mail-boats and slave-ships both, go twice a month, and the number of slaves exported by them yearly has lately averaged a little under four thousand, though the numbers are increasing, as I showed in my last letter.

The slaves are, of course, kept in the fore part of the ship. All day long they lie about the lower deck,

[1] See note on page 185.

among the horses, mules, cattle, sheep, monkeys, and other live-stock; or they climb up to the fo'c's'le deck in hopes of getting a little breeze, and it is there that the mothers chiefly lie beside their tiny babies. There is nothing to do. Hardly any one speaks, and over the faces of nearly all broods the look of dumb bewilderment that one sees in cattle crowded into trucks for the slaughter-market. Twice a day rations of mealy pap or brown beans are issued in big pots. Each pot is supplied with ten wooden spoons and holds the food for ten slaves, who have to get as much of it as each can manage. The first-class passengers, leaning against the rail of the upper deck, look down upon the scene with interest and amusement. To them those slaves represent the secret of Portugal's greatness—such greatness as Portugal has.

At sunset they are herded into a hold, the majority going down the hatchway stairs on their hands and knees. There they spread their sleeping-mats, and the hatch is shut down upon them till the following morning. By the virtuous Decree of 1903, which regulates the transport, "the emigrants [*i.e.*, the slaves] shall be separated according to sex into completely isolated compartments, and may not sleep on deck, nor resume conjugal relations before leaving the ship." Certainly the slaves do not sleep on deck, but as to the other clauses I have seen no attempt to carry out the regulations, ex-

cept such measures as the slaves take themselves
by dividing the hold between men and women. It
may seem strange, but all my observation has shown
me that, in spite of nakedness and the absence of
shame in most natural affairs of existence, the natives are far more particular about the really important matters of sex than civilized people are;
just as most animals are far more particular, and
for the same reasons. I mean that for them the
difference of sex is mainly a matter of livelihood
and child-getting, not of casual debauchery.

Even a coast trader said to me one evening, as
we were looking down into the hold where the slaves
were arranging their mats, "What a different thing
if they were white people!"

The day after leaving Benguela we stopped off
Novo Redondo to take on more cargo. The slaves
came off in two batches—fifty in the morning and
thirty more towards sunset. There was a bit of a
sea on that day, and the tossing of the lighter had
made most of the slaves very sick. Things became
worse when the lighter lay rising and falling with
the waves at the foot of the gangway, and the slaves
had to be dragged up to the platform one by one
like sacks, and set to climb the ladder as best they
could. I remember especially one poor woman who
held in her arms a baby only two or three days old.
Quickly as native women recover from childbirth,
she had hardly recovered, and was very sea-sick

besides. In trying to reach the platform, she kept on missing the rise of the wave, and was flung violently back again into the lighter. At last the men managed to haul her up and set her on the foot of the ladder, striking her sharply to make her mount. Tightening the cloth that held the baby to her back, and gathering up her dripping blanket over one arm, she began the ascent on all-fours. Almost at once her knees caught in the blanket and she fell flat against the sloping stairs. In that position she wriggled up them like a snake, clutching at each stair with her arms above her head. At last she reached the top, bruised and bleeding, soaked with water, her blanket lost, most of her gaudy clothing torn off or hanging in strips. On her back the little baby, still crumpled and almost pink from the womb, squeaked feebly like a blind kitten. But swinging it round to her breast, the woman walked modestly and without complaint to her place in the row with the others.

I have heard many terrible sounds, but never anything so hellish as the outbursts of laughter with which the ladies and gentlemen of the first class watched that slave woman's struggle up to the deck.

When all the slaves were on board at last, a steward or one of the ship's officers mustered them in a row, and the ship's doctor went down the line to perform the medical examination, in accordance with Chapter VI. of the Decree, enacting that no diseased or infectious person shall be accepted. It is entirely to the doctor's interest to foster the health of the slaves, for, as I have already mentioned, every death loses him two shillings. As a rule, as I have said, he loses four per cent. of his cargo, or two dollars out of every possible fifty. On this particular voyage, however, he was more fortunate, for only two slaves out of the whole number died during the week, and were thrown overboard during the first-class breakfast-hour, so that the feelings of the passengers might not be harrowed.

Next day after leaving Novo Redondo we reached Loanda and increased our cargo by forty-two men and women, all tricked out in the most amazing tartan plaids—the tartans of Israel in the Highlands. This made up our total number of two hundred and seventy-two, not reckoning babies, which, unhappily, I did not count. Probably there were about fifty. I think neither the captain nor the doctor receives any percentage for landing babies alive, but, of course, if they live to grow up on the plantations, which is very seldom, they become even more valuable than the imported adults, and the planter gets them gratis.

Early next morning, when we were anchored off Ambriz, a commotion suddenly arose on board, and the rumor ran that one of the slaves had jumped into the sea from the bow. Soon we could see his black head as he swam clear of the ship and struck out southwards, apparently trusting to the current to bear him towards the coast. For he was a native of a village near Ambriz and knew what he was about. It was yearning at the sight of his own land that made him run the risk. The sea was full of sharks, and I could only hope that they might devour him before man could seize him again. Already a boat had been hastily dropped into the water and was in pursuit, manned by two black men and a white. They rowed fast over the oily water, and the swimmer struggled on in vain. The chase lasted barely ten minutes and they were upon him. Leaning over the side of the boat, they battered him with oars and sticks till he was quiet. Then they dragged him into the boat, laid him along the bottom, and stretched a piece of old sail over his nakedness, that the ladies might not be shocked. He was brought to the gangway and dragged, dripping and trembling, up the stairs. The doctor and the government Agent, who accompanies each shipload of slaves, took him down into the hold, and there he was chained up to a post or staple so that he might cause no trouble again. "Flog him! Flog him! A good flogging!" cried the passengers. "Boa chicote!" I have not the slightest doubt he was flogged without mercy, but if so, it was kept secret —an unnecessary waste of pleasure, for the passengers would thoroughly have enjoyed both the sight and sound of the lashing. The comfortable and educated classes in all nations appear not to have altered in the least since the days when the comfortable and educated classes of Paris used to arrange promenades to see the Communards shot in batches against a wall. They may whine and blubber over imaginary sufferings in novels and plays, but touch their comfort, touch their property —they are rattlesnakes then!

We stopped at Cabinda in the Portuguese territory north of the Congo, and at one or two other trading-places on the coast, and then we put out northwest for the islands. On the eighth day after leaving Benguela we came in sight of San Thomé. Over it the sky was a broken gray of drifting rain-clouds. Only now and again we could see the high peaks of the mountains, which run up to seven thousand feet. The valleys at their base were shrouded in the pale and drizzling mists which hang about them almost continually. Here and there a rounded hill, indigo with forest, rose from the mists and showed us the white house of some plantation and the little cluster of out-buildings and huts where the slaves were to find their new home. Then, as on an enchanted island, the ghostly fog stole over it again, and in another quarter some fresh hill, indigo with forest, stood revealed.

The whole place smoked and steamed like a gigantic hot-house. In fact, it is a gigantic hot-house. As nearly as possible, it stands upon the equator, the actual line passing through the volcanic rocks of its southern extremity. And even in the dry season from April to October it is perpetually soaked with moisture. The wet mist hardly ceases to hang among the hills and forest trees. The thick growth of the tropics covers the mountains almost to their summits, and every leaf of verdure drips with warm dew.

The slaves on deck regarded the scene with almost complete apathy. Some of the men leaned against the bulwark and silently watched the points of the island as we passed. The women hardly stirred from their places. They were occupied with their babies as usual, or lay about in the unbroken wretchedness of despair. Two girls of about fifteen or sixteen, evidently sisters, whom I had before noticed for a certain pathetic beauty, now sat huddled together hand-in-hand, quietly crying. They were just the kind of girls that the planters select for their concubines, and I have little doubt they are the concubines of planters now. But they cried because they feared they would be separated when they came to land.

In the confusion of casting anchor I stood by them unobserved, and in a low voice asked them a few questions in Umbundu, which I had crammed up for the purpose. The answers were brief, in

sobbing whispers; sometimes by gestures only. The
conversation ran like this:

"Why are you here?"
"We were sold to the white men."
"Did you come of your own free will?"
"Of course not."
"Where did you come from?"
"From Bihé."
"Are you slaves or not?"
"Of course we are slaves!"
"Would you like to go back?"

The delicate little brown hands were stretched out,
palms downward, and the crying began afresh.

That night the slaves were left on board, but next
morning (June 17th) when I went down to the pier
about nine o'clock, I found them being landed in
two great lighters. One by one the men and women
were dragged up on to the pier by their arms and
loin-cloths and dumped down like bales of goods.
There they sat in four lines till all were ready, and
then, carrying their mats and babies, they were
marched off in file to the Curador's house in the
town beside the bay. Here they were driven through
large iron gates into a court-yard and divided up
into gangs according to the names of the planters
who had requisitioned for them. When the parties
were complete, they were put under the charge of
gangers belonging to various plantations, and so
they set out on foot upon the last stage of their

journey. When they reached their plantation (which would usually be on the same day or the next, for the island is only thirty-five miles long by fifteen broad) they would be given a day or two for rest, and then the daily round of labor would begin. For them there are no more journeyings, till that last short passage when their dead bodies are lashed to poles and carried out to be flung away in the forest.

NOTE.—I have no direct evidence that the poison was given me intentionally, but the "cumulative" evidence is rather strong. While still in the interior I had been warned that the big slave-dealers had somehow got to know of my purpose and were plotting against me. On the coast the warnings increased, till my life became almost as ludicrous as a melodrama, and I was obliged to "live each day as 'twere my last"—an unpleasant and unprofitable mode of living. One man would drop hints, another would give instances of Portuguese treachery. I was often told the fate of a poor Portuguese trader named De Silva, who objected to slavery and was going to Lisbon to expose the system, but after his first meal on board was found dead in his cabin. People in the street whispered of my fate. A restaurant-keeper at Benguela told an English fellow-passenger on my ship that he had better not be seen with me, for I was in great danger. My boy, who had followed me right through from the Gold Coast with the fidelity of a homeless dog, kept bringing me rumors of murder that he heard among the natives. Two nights before the ship sailed I was at a dinner given by the engineers of the new railway, and into my overcoat-pocket some one, whom I wish publicly to thank, tucked a scrap of paper with the words, "You are in great peril," written in French. If there was a plot to set upon me in the empty streets that night, it was prevented by an Englishman who volunteered to go back with me, though I had not told him of any danger. Next night I was poisoned. Owing to the frequent warnings, I was ready with antidotes, but I think I should not have reached the ship alive next day without the courageous and devoted help of a South-African prospector who had been shut up with me in Ladysmith. The Dutch trader with whom I was staying was himself far above suspicion, but I shall not forget his indignant excitement when he saw what had happened. Evidently it was what he had feared, though I only told him I must have eaten something unwholesome. The tiresome sense of apprehension lasted during my voyage to the islands, and I was obliged to keep a dyspeptic watch upon the food. But I do not wish to make much of these little personal matters. To American and English people in their security they naturally seem absurd, and as a proof how common the art of poisoning still is in Portuguese possessions I will only mention that I have met a Portuguese trader in San Thomé who carries about in his waistcoat a little packet of pounded glass which he detected one evening in his soup, and that on the Portuguese ship which finally took me from San Thomé to Lisbon a Portuguese official died the day we started, from an illness due to his belief that he was being poisoned, and that during the voyage a poor Belgian from the interior gradually faded away under the same belief, and was carried out at Lisbon in a dying condition. Of course both may have been mad, but even madness does not take that form without something to suggest it.

X

LIFE OF SLAVES ON THE ISLANDS

THEY stand in the Gulf of Guinea—those two islands of San Thomé and Principe where the slaves die—about one hundred and fifty miles from the nearest coast at the Gaboon River in French Congo. San Thomé lies just above the equator, Principe some eighty miles north and a little east of San Thomé, and a hundred and twenty miles southwest of Fernando Po. San Thomé is about eight times as large as Principe, and the population, which may now be reckoned considerably over forty thousand, is also about eight times as large. It is difficult to say what proportion of these populations are slaves. The official returns of 1900 put the population of San Thomé at 37,776, including 19,211 serviçaes, or slaves, with an import of 4572 serviçaes in 1901. And the population of Principe was given as 4327, including 3175 serviçaes. But the prosperity of the islands is increasing with such rapidity that these numbers have now been probably far surpassed.[1]

[1] An English resident at San Thomé estimates the serviçaes alone at forty thousand.

It is cocoa that has created the prosperity. In
old days the islands were famous for their coffee,
and it is still perhaps the best in Africa. But the
trade in coffee sank to less than a half in the ten
years, 1891 to 1901, while in that time the cocoa
trade increased fourfold—from 3597 tons to 14,914
—and since 1901 the increase has been still more
rapid. The islands possess exactly the kind of
climate that kills men and makes the cocoa-tree
flourish. It is, as I have described, a hot-house climate—burning heat and torrents of rain in the wet
season, from October to April; stifling heat and
clouds of dripping mist in the season that is called
dry. In such an air and upon the fine volcanic soil
the cocoa-plant thrives wherever it is set, and continues to produce all the year round. Nearly one-
third of the islands is now under cultivation, and the
wild forest is constantly being cleared away. In
consequence, the value of land has gone up beyond
the dreams of a land-grabber's avarice. Little plots
that could be had for the asking ten years ago now
fetch their hundreds. There is a story, perhaps
mythical, that one of the greatest owners—once a
clerk or carrier in San Thomé—has lately refused
£2,000,000 for his plantations there. In 1901 the
export trade from San Thomé alone was valued at
£764,830, having more than doubled in five years,
and by this time it is certainly over £1,000,000.
There are probably about two hundred and thirty

plantations or "roças" on San Thomé now, some employing as many as one thousand slaves. And on Principe there are over fifty roças, with from three hundred to five hundred slaves working upon the largest. All these evidences of increasing prosperity must be very satisfactory to the private proprietors and to the shareholders in the companies which own a large proportion of the land. For the most part they live in Lisbon, enjoying themselves upon the product of the cocoa-tree and the lives of men and women.

One early morning at San Thomé I went out to visit a plantation which is rightly regarded as a kind of model—a show-place for the intelligent foreigner or for the Portuguese shareholder who feels qualms as he banks his dividends. There were four hundred slaves on the estate, not counting children, and I was shown their neat brick huts in rows, quite recently finished. I saw them clearing the forest for further plantation, clearing the ground under the cocoa-trees, gathering the great yellow pods, sorting the brown kernels, which already smelled like a chocolate-box, heaping them up to ferment, raking them out in vast pans to dry, working in the carpenters' sheds, superintending the new machines, and gathering in groups for the mid-day meal. I was shown the turbine engine, the electric light, the beautiful wood-work in the manager's house, the clean and roomy hospital with its copious supply of drugs and anatomical curiosities in bottles, the isolated house for infectious cases. To an outward seeming, the Decree of 1903 for the regulation of the slave labor had been carried out in every possible respect. All looked as perfect and legal as an English industrial school. Then we sat down to an exquisite Parisian *déjeuner* under the bower of a drooping tree, and while I was meditating on the hardships of African travel, a saying of another of the guests kept coming back to my mind: "The Portuguese are certainly doing a marvellous work for Angola and these islands. Call it slavery if you like. Names and systems don't matter. The sum of human happiness is being infinitely increased."

The doctor had come up to pay his official visit to the plantation that day. "The death-rate on this roça," he remarked, casually, during the meal, "is twelve or fourteen per cent. a year among the serviçaes." "And what is the chief cause?" I asked. "Anæmia," he said. "That is a vague sort of thing," I answered; "what brings on anæmia?" "Unhappiness [tristeza]," he said, frankly.

He went on to explain that if they could keep a slave alive for three or four years from the date of landing, he generally lived some time longer, but it was very difficult to induce them to live through the misery and homesickness of the first few years.

This cause, however, does not account for the high mortality among the children. On one of the largest and best-managed plantations of San Thomé the superintendent admits a children's death-rate of twenty-five per cent., or one-quarter of all the children, every year. Our latest consular reports do not give a complete return of the death-rate for San Thomé, but on Principe 867 slaves died during 1901 (491 males and 376 females), which gives a total death-rate of 20.67 per cent. per annum. In other words, you may calculate that among the slaves on Principe one in every five will be dead by the end of the year.[1]

No wonder that the price of slaves is high, and that it is almost impossible for the supply from Angola to keep pace with the demand, though the government calls on its Agents to drive the trade as hard as they can, and the Agents do their very utmost to encourage the natives to raid, kidnap, accuse of witchcraft, press for debts, soak in rum, and sell. A manager in Principe, who employs one hundred and fifty slaves on his roça, told me that it is impossible for him fully to develop the land without two hundred more, but he simply cannot afford the £6000 needed for the purchase of that number.

The common saying that if you have seen one

---

[1] London's death-rate in 1903 was 15.7 per 1000 against Principe's 206.7 per 1000. Liverpool had the highest death-rate of English cities. It was 20.5 per 1000, or almost exactly one-tenth of the death-rate among the serviçaes in Principe. The total death-rate for England and Wales in 1902 was 16.2 per 1000.

plantation you have seen all is not exactly true. I found the plantations differed a good deal according to the wealth of the proprietor and the superintendent's disposition. Still there is a general similarity in external things from which one can easily build up a type. Let us take, for instance, a roça which I visited one Sunday after driving some six or seven miles into the interior from the port of San Thomé. The road led through groves of the cocoa-tree, the gigantic "cotton-tree," breadfruit, palms, and many hard and useful woods which I did not know. For a great part of the distance the wild and untouched forest stood thick on both sides, and as we climbed into the mountains we looked down into unpenetrated glades, where parrots, monkeys, and civet-cats are the chief inhabitants. The sides of the road were thickly covered with moss and fern, and the high rocks and tree-tops were from time to time concealed by the soaking white mist which the people for some strange reason call "flying-fish milk." High up in the hills we came to a filthy village, where a few slaves were drearily lying about, full of the deadly rum that hardly even cheers. A few hundred yards farther up was the roça which owns the village and runs the rum-shop there for the benefit of the slaves and its own pocket. The buildings are arranged in a great quadrangle, with high walls all round and big gates that are locked at night. On one side

stands the planter's house, and attached to it are
the dwellings of the overseers, or gangers, together
with the quarters of such slaves as are employed
for domestic purposes, whether as concubines or
servants. On the other side stand the quarters of
the ordinary slaves who labor on the plantation.
They are built in long sheds, and in a few cases
these are two stories high, but in most plantations
only one. Some of the sheds are arranged like the
dormitories in our barracks; sometimes the homes
are almost or entirely isolated; sometimes, as in this
roça, they are divided by partitions, like the stalls
in a stable. At one end of the quadrangle, besides
the magazines for the working and storage of the
cocoa, there is a huge barn, which the slaves use as
a kitchen, each family making its own little fire on
the ground and cooking its rations separately, as
the unconquerable habit of all natives is. At the
other end of the quadrangle, sunk below the level
of the fall of the hill, stands the hospital, with its
male and female wards duly divided according to
law.

The centre of the quadrangle is occupied by great
flat pans, paved with cement or stones, for the dry-
ing of the cocoa-beans. Within the largest of these
enclosures the slaves are gathered two or three times
a week to receive their rations of meal and dried
fish. At six o'clock on the afternoon of my visit
they all assembled to the clanging of the bell, the

grown-up slaves bringing large bundles of grass, which they had gathered as part of their daily task, for the mules and cattle. They stood round the edges of the square in perfect silence. In the centre of the square at regular intervals stood the whity-brown gangers, leaning on their long sticks or flicking their boots with whips. Beside them lay the large and savage dogs which prowl round the buildings at night to prevent the slaves escaping in the darkness. As it was Sunday afternoon, the slaves were called upon to enjoy the Sunday treat. First came the children one by one, and to each of them was given a little sup of wine from a pitcher. Then the square began slowly to move round in single file. Slabs of dried fish were given out as rations, and for the special Sunday treat each man or woman received two leaves of raw tobacco from one of the superintendent's mistresses, or, if they preferred it, one leaf of tobacco and a sup of wine in a mug. Nearly all chose the two leaves of tobacco as the more lasting joy. When they had received their dole, they passed round the square again in single file, till all had made the circuit. From first to last not a single word was spoken. It was more like a military execution than a festival.

About once a month the slaves receive their wages in a similar manner. By the Decree of 1903, the minimum wage for a man is fixed at 2500 reis (something under ten shillings) a month, and for a woman at 1800 reis. But, as a matter of fact, the planters tell me that the average wage is 1200 reis a month, or about one and twopence a week. In some cases the wages are higher, and one or two slaves were pointed out to me whose wages came to fifteen shillings a month. I am told that in the islands, unlike the custom on the mainland, these wages are really paid in cash and not by tokens, but the planters always add that as the money can only be spent in the plantation store, nearly all of it comes back to them in the form of profit on rum or cloth or food.

According to the law, only two-fifths of the wages are to be paid every month, the remaining three-fifths going to a "Repatriation Fund" in San Thomé. In the case of the slaves from Angola this is never done, and it is much to the credit of the Portuguese that, as there is no repatriation, they have dropped the institution of a Repatriation Fund. They might easily have pocketed three-fifths of the slaves' wages under that excuse, but this advantage they have renounced. They never send the slaves home, and they do not deduct the money for doing it. Neither do they deduct a proportion of the wages which, according to the law, might be sent to the mainland for the support of a man's family till the termination of his contract. They know a contract terminates only at death, and from this easy method of swindling they also abstain. It is, as I said, to their credit, the more because it is so unlike their custom.

For some reason which I do not quite understand —perhaps because they come under French government—the Cape Verde serviçaes receive a higher wage (three thousand reis for a man and twenty-five hundred for a woman); about a third is deducted every month for repatriation, and in many cases, at all events, the people are actually sent back. So the planters told me, though I have not seen them on a returning ship myself.

According to the law, the wages of all slaves must be raised ten per cent. if they agree to renew their contract for a second term of five years. With the best will in the world, it would be almost impossible to carry out this provision, for no slave ever does agree to renew his contract. His wishes in the matter are no more consulted than a blind horse's in a coal-pit. The owner or Agent of the plantation waits till the five years of about fifty of his slaves have expired. Then he sends for the Curador from San Thomé, and lines up the fifty in front of him. In the presence of two witnesses and his secretary the Curador solemnly announces to the slaves that the term of their contract is up and the contract is renewed for five years more. The slaves are then dismissed and another scene in the cruel farce of contracted labor is over. One of the planters told me that he thought some of his slaves counted the years for the first five, but never afterwards.

Some planters do not even go through the form of bringing the Curador and the time-expired slaves face to face. They simply send down the papers for signature, and do not mention the matter to the slaves at all. At the end of June, 1905, a planter told me he had sent down the papers in April and had not yet received them back. He was getting a little anxious. "Of course," he said, "it makes no difference whatever to the slaves. They know nothing about it. But I like to comply with the law."

In one respect, however, that well-intentioned citizen did not comply with the law at all. The law lays it down that every owner of fifty slaves must set up a hospital with separate wards for the sexes. This man employed nearly two hundred slaves and had no hospital at all. The official doctor came up and visited the sick in their crowded huts twice a month.

The law lays it down that a crèche shall be kept on each plantation for children under seven, and certainly I have seen the little black infants herding about in the dust together among the empty huts while their parents were at work. Children are not allowed to be driven to work before they are eleven, and up to fourteen they may be compelled to do only certain kinds of labor. From fourteen to sixteen two kinds of labor are excluded —cutting timber and trenching the coffee. After sixteen they become full-grown slaves, and may be forced to do any kind of work. These provisions are only legal, but, as I noticed before, the children born on a plantation, if only they can be kept alive to maturity, ought to make the most valuable kind of slaves. Their keep has cost very little, and otherwise they come to the planter for nothing, like all good gifts of God. This is what makes me doubt the truth of a story one often hears about San Thomé, that a woman who is found to be with child after landing is flogged to death in the presence of the others. It is not the cruelty that makes me question it. Give a lonely white man absolute authority over blacks, and there is no length to which his cruelty may not go. But the loss in cash would be too considerable. At landing, a woman has cost the planter as much as two cows, and no good business man would flog a cow to death because she was in calf.

The same considerations tend, of course, to prevent all violent acts of cruelty such as might bring death. The cost of slaves is so large, the demand is so much greater than the supply, and the death-rate is so terrible in any case that a good planter's first thought is to do all he can to keep his stock of slaves alive. It is true that in most men passion easily overcomes interest, and for an outsider it is impossible to judge of such things. When a stranger is coming, the word goes round that everything must be made to look as smooth and pleasant as possible. No one can realize the inner truth of the slave's life unless he has lived many years on the plantations. But I am inclined to think that for business reasons the violent forms of cruelty are unlikely and uncommon. Flogging, however, is common if not universal, and so are certain forms of vice. The prettiest girls are chosen by the Agents and gangers as their concubines — that is natural. But it was worse when a planter pointed me out a little boy and girl of about seven or eight, and boasted that like most of the children they were already instructed in acts of bestiality, the contemplation of which seemed to give him a pleasing amusement amid the brutalizing tedium of a planter's life.

In spite of all precautions and the boasted comfort of their lot, some of the slaves succeed in escaping. On San Thomé they generally take to highway robbery, and white men always go armed in consequence. The law decrees that a recaptured runaway is to be restored to his owner, and after the customary flogging he is then set to work again. Sometimes the runaways are hunted and shot down. On one of the mountains of San Thomé, I am told, you may still see a heap of bones where a party of runaway slaves were shot, but I have not seen them myself. For some reason, perhaps because of the greater wildness of the island, there are many more runaways on Principe, small as it is. The place is like a magic land, the dream of some wild painter. Points of cliff run sheer up from the sea, and between them lie secret little bays where a boat may be pushed off quietly over the sand. In one such bay, where the dense forest comes right down to the beach, a long canoe was gradually scooped out in January (1905) and filled with provisions for a voyage. When all was ready, eighteen escaped slaves launched it by night and paddled away into the darkness of the sea. For many days and nights they toiled, ignorant of all direction. They only knew that somewhere across the sea was their home. But before their provisions were quite spent, the current and the powers of evil that watch over slaves bore them to the coast of Fernando Po. Thinking they had reached freedom at last, they crept out of the boat on to the welcome shore, and there the authorities seized upon them, and, to the endless shame of Spain, packed them all on a steamer and sent them back in a single day to the place from which they came.

That is one of the things that make us anarchists. Probably there was hardly any one on Fernando Po, though it is a slave island itself, who would not willingly have saved those men if he had been left to his own instincts. But directly the state authority came in, their cause was hopeless. So it is that wherever you touch government you seem to touch the devil.

The eighteen were taken back to Principe, flogged almost to death in the jail, returned to their owners, and any of them who survive are still at work on the plantations, with but the memory of that brief happiness and overwhelming defeat to think upon.

When escaping slaves have reached the Cameroons, the Germans resolutely refuse to give them back, and by that refusal they have done much to cover the errors and harshness of their own colonial system. What would happen now to slaves who reached Nigeria or the Gold Coast, one hardly dares to think. There was a time when we used to hear fine stories of slaves falling on the beach when they touched British territory and kissing the soil of freedom. But that was long ago, and since then England has grown rich and fallen from her high estate. Her hands are no longer clean, and when people think of Johannesburg and Queensland and western Australia, all she may say of freedom becomes an empty sound, impressing no one.

Last April (1905) another of the planters discovered a party of eight of his own slaves just launching a canoe in hopes of escaping with better success. They had crammed the canoe with provisions—slaughtered pigs, meal, and water-casks—so many things that the planter told me it would certainly have sunk and drowned them all. To prevent this lamentable catastrophe he took them to the jail, had them flogged almost to death by the jailer there, and brought them back to the huts which they had so rashly attempted to leave in spite of their legal contract and their supposed willingness to work on the plantations.

In the interior, the island of Principe rises into great peaks, not so high as the mountains of San Thomé, but very much more precipitous. There is one peak especially where the rock falls so sheer that I think it would be inaccessible to the best climber on that side. I have not discovered the exact height of the mountains, but I should estimate them as something between four and five thousand feet, and they, like the whole island, are covered with forest and tropical growth, except where the rock is too steep and smooth to give any hold for roots. But, as a rule, one sees the mountains only by glimpses, for when I have passed the island or landed there they have always been wrapped in slowly moving mist, and I believe they are seldom clear of it. The mist falls in a soaking drizzle, and it seems to rain heavily, besides, almost every day, even in the dry season. Perhaps the moisture is almost too great, for I noticed more rot upon the cocoa-pods here than at San Thomé.

Into these dripping forests and almost inaccessible mountains the slaves are constantly trying to escape. A planter told me that many of them do not realize what an island is. They hope to be able to make their way home on foot. When they discover that the terrible sea foams all round them, they turn into the forest and build little huts, from which they are continually moving away. Here and there they plant little patches of maize or other food with seed which they steal from the plantations or which is secretly conveyed to them by the other slaves. Some kind of communication is evidently kept up, for it is thought the plantation slaves always know where the runaways are, and sometimes betray them. I saw one man who had been living with them in the forest himself and had come back with his hand cut off and his head split open, probably for treachery. We asked him the reason; we asked him to tell us something of the life out there; but at once he assumed the native's impenetrable look and would not speak another word.

Women as well as men escape from time to time and join these fine vindicators of freedom in the woods, but, chiefly owing to the deadly climate and the extreme hardship of their life, the people do not increase in numbers. About a thousand was the highest figure I heard given for them; about two hundred the lowest. The number most generally quoted was six hundred, but, in fact, it is quite impossible to count them at all, for they are always changing their camps and are rarely seen.

The cotton cloths in which they escape go to pieces very soon, and they all live in entire nakedness, except when the women take the trouble to string together a few plantain leaves as aprons. Among them, however, they have some clever craftsmen. They make good bows and arrows for hunting the civet-cats and other animals that form their chief food, and I have seen a two-handled saw made out of a common knife or matchet—a very ingenious piece of work. It was found in the hands of one of them who had been shot.

For the most part they live a wandering and hard, but I hope not an entirely unhappy, existence in the dense forest around the base of that precipitous mountain of which I spoke. Every now and again the Portuguese organize man-hunts to recapture or kill them off. Forming a kind of cordon, they sweep over parts of the island, tying up or shooting all they may find. But the Portuguese are so cowardly and incapable in their undertakings that they are no match for alert natives filled with the recklessness of despair, and the massacre has never yet been complete. In fact, the hunting-parties are often broken up by dissensions among rival strategists, and sometimes they appear to degenerate into convivial meetings, at which drink is the object and murder the excuse.

Recently, however, there was a very successful shoot. The sportsmen had been led by guides to a place where the escaped slaves were known to be rather thick in the forest. They came upon huts evidently just abandoned. Beside them, hidden in the grass, they found an old man. "We took him," said the planter who told me the story, with all a sportsman's relish, "and we forced him to tell us where the others were. At first we could not squeeze a word or sign out of him. After a long time, without saying anything, he lifted a hand towards the highest trees, and there we saw the slaves, men and women, clinging like bats to the under side of the branches. It was not long, I can tell you, before we brought them crashing down through the leaves on to the ground. My word, we had grand sport that day!"

I can imagine no more noble existence than has fallen to those poor and naked blacks, who have dared all for freedom, and, scorning the stall-fed life of slavery, have chosen rather to throw themselves upon such mercy as nature has, to wander together in nakedness and hunger from forest to forest and hut to hut, to live in daily apprehension of murder, to lurk like apes under the high branches, and at last to fall to the bullets of the Christians, dead, but of no further service to the commercial gentlemen who bought them and lose £30 by every death.

Even to the slaves who remain on the plantations, not having the courage or good-fortune to escape and die like wild beasts, death, as a rule, is not much longer delayed in coming. Probably within the first two or three years the slave's strength begins to ebb away. With every day his work becomes feebler, so that at last even the ganger's whip or pointed stick cannot urge him on. Then he is taken to the hospital and laid upon the boarded floor till he dies. An hour or so afterwards you may meet two of his fellow-slaves going into the forest. There is perhaps a sudden smell of carbolic or other disinfectant upon the air, and you take another look at the long pole the slaves are carrying between them on their shoulders. Under the pole a body is lashed, tightly wrapped up in the cotton cloth that was its dress while it lived. The head is covered with another piece of cloth which passes round the neck and is also fastened tightly to the pole. The feet and legs are sometimes covered, sometimes left to dangle naked. In silence the two slaves pass into some untrodden part of the forest, and the man or woman who started on life's journey in a far-off native village with the average hope and delight of childhood, travels over the last brief stage and is no more seen.

Laws and treaties do not count for much. A law is never of much effect unless the mind of a people has passed beyond the need of it, and treaties are binding only on those who wish to be bound. But still there are certain laws and treaties that we may for a moment recall: in 1830 England paid £300,000 to the Portuguese provided they forbade all slave-trade—which they did and pocketed the money; in 1842 England and the United States agreed under the Ashburton Treaty to maintain joint squadrons on the west coast of Africa for the suppression of the slave-trade; in 1858 Portugal enacted a law that every slave belonging to a Portuguese subject should be free in twenty years; in 1885, by the Berlin General Act, England, the United States, and thirteen other powers, including Portugal and Belgium, pledged themselves to suppress every kind of slave-trade, especially in the Congo and the interior of Africa; in 1890, by the Brussels General Act, England, the United States, and fifteen other powers, including Portugal and Belgium, pledged themselves to suppress every kind of slave-trade, especially in the Congo and the interior of Africa, to erect cities of refuge for escaped slaves, to hold out protection to every fugitive slave, to stop all convoys of slaves on the march, and to exercise strict supervision at all ports so as to prevent the sale or shipment of slaves across the sea.

If any one wanted a theme for satire, what more deadly theme could he find?

To which of the powers can appeal now be made? Appeal to England is no longer possible. Since the rejection of Ireland's home-rule bill, the abandonment of the Armenians to massacre, and the extinction of the South-African republics, she can no longer be regarded as the champion of liberty or of justice among mankind. She has flung away her only noble heritage. She has closed her heart of compassion, and for ten years past the oppressed have called to her in vain. A single British cruiser, posted off the coast of Angola, with orders to arrest every mail-boat or other ship having serviçaes on board, would so paralyze the system that probably it would never recover. But one might as soon expect Russia or Germany to do it as England in her recent mood. She will make representations, perhaps; she will remind Portugal of "the old alliance" and the friendship between the royal families; but she will do no more. What she says can have no effect; her tongue, which was the tongue of men, has become like sounding brass; and if she spoke of freedom, the nations would listen with a polished smile.

From her we can turn only to America. There the sense of freedom still seems to linger, and the people are still capable of greater actions than can ever be prompted by commercial interests and the search for a market. America's record is still clean compared to England's, and her impulses to compassion and justice will not be checked by family affection for the royalties of one out of the two most degraded, materialized, and unintellectual lit-

tle states of Europe. America may still take the
part that once was England's by right of inheri-
tance. She may stand as the bulwark of freedom
against tyranny, and of justice and mercy—those
almost extinct qualities—against the restless greed
and blood - thirsty pleasure - seeking of the world.
Let America declare that her will is set against
slavery, and at her voice the abominable trade in
human beings between Angola and the islands will
collapse as the slave-trade to Brazil collapsed at
the voice of England in the days of her greatness.

I am aware that, as I said in my first letter, the
whole question of slavery is still before us. It
has reappeared under the more pleasing names of
"indentured labor," "contract labor," or the "com-
pulsory labor" which Mr. Chamberlain has ad-
vocated in obedience to the Johannesburg mine-
owners. The whole thing will have to be faced anew,
for the solutions of our great-grandfathers no longer
satisfy. While slavery is lucrative, as it is on the
islands of San Thomé and Principe, it will be de-
fended by those who identify greatness with wealth,
and if their own wealth is involved, their arguments will gain considerably in vigor. They will
point to the necessity of developing rich islands
where no one would work without compulsion.
They will point to what they call the comfort and
good treatment of the slaves. They will protect
themselves behind legal terms. But they forget

that legal terms make no difference to the truth of things. They forget that slavery is not a matter of discomfort or ill treatment, but of loss of liberty. They forget that it might be better for mankind that the islands should go back to wilderness than that a single slave should toil there. I know the contest is still before us. It is but part of the great contest with capitalism, and in Africa it will be as long and difficult as it was a hundred years ago in other regions of the world. I have but tried to reveal one small glimpse in a greater battle-field, and to utter the cause of a few thousands out of the millions of men and women whose silence is heard only by God. And perhaps if the crying of their silence is not heard even by God, it will yet be heard in the souls of the just and the compassionate.

INDEX

INDEX

INDEX

Date Due
